DRILL HERE
DRILL NOW
PAY LESS

DRILL HERE
DRILL NOW
PAY LESS

A HANDBOOK FOR SLASHING GAS PRICES AND SOLVING OUR ENERGY CRISIS

NEWT GINGRICH

WITH VINCE HALEY

Since 1947
REGNERY
PUBLISHING, INC.
An Eagle Publishing Company • Washington, DC

Cataloging-in-Publication Data on file with the Library of Congress
ISBN 978–1–59698–576–6

Published in the United States by
Regnery Publishing, Inc.
One Massachusetts Avenue, NW
Washington, DC 20001
www.regnery.com

Manufactured in the United States of America
10 9 8 7 6 5 4 3 2 1

Books are available in quantity for promotional or premium use. Write to Director of Special Sales, Regnery Publishing, Inc., One Massachusetts Avenue NW, Washington, DC 20001, for information on discounts and terms or call (202) 216-0600.

This book is dedicated to every American whose family finances are strained or whose job is threatened by an absolutely unnecessary energy crisis.

The printer of the cover of this book is certified as meeting the Forest Stewardship Council's principles and criteria for forest management.

CONTENTS

WHY I WROTE THIS BOOK

America is suffering from an artificial energy crisis that is also a dangerous national security crisis—artificial, because America is gifted with enormous reserves of energy; dangerous, because it makes us vulnerable to unreliable and potentially hostile countries.

With oil prices skyrocketing, electricity costs rising, and the American people rightly outraged at soaring gas prices and our dependence on foreign oil, how did our government respond?

The U.S. Senate was so out of touch with the people who elected it that it considered a bill to make energy more expensive.

The Senate debated this past June—and at one point seemed ready to pass—not a pro-energy bill but an anti-energy bill. Called the Boxer-Warner-Lieberman bill, it would have restricted the domestic supply of energy even more and effectively increased the federal tax on gasoline, diesel, and other fuels and energy supplies.

The Boxer amendment alone would have raised the price of gas by $1 per gallon at a time when family budgets were already being wrecked by high gas prices.

To state the obvious, current American energy policy is a disaster—and our government isn't doing anything about it. It's time for we the people to act.

DRILL HERE, DRILL NOW, PAY LESS

I decided the first step was to launch a petition drive. So far, more than 1.4 million people have signed our "Drill Here, Drill Now, Pay Less" petition at www.AmericanSolutions.com, and the number grows every day.

Chuck Norris created a YouTube video supporting our Drill Here, Drill Now, Pay Less theme, and hundreds of thousands of people have seen it.

I did a similar video on three ways to lower the price of gas and it spread rapidly, with more than 2.6 million viewers.

And we began to see political action.

Senator McCain came out for offshore drilling, and Governor Charlie Crist of Florida called for drilling off the Florida coast. President Bush repealed the eighteen-year-old executive order banning offshore drilling.

Congressman Lyn Westmoreland launched a petition drive for more American energy production and got nearly 200 members of the U.S. House of Representatives—both Democrats and Republicans—to sign up. (It only takes 218 members to win a vote, so he's getting close.)

With these efforts and others—including this book—we are gaining momentum to enact a fundamentally new and more effective energy policy that will save us money, improve our national security, and enhance our efforts to protect the environment.

The fact is, we have more energy resources than any other country in the world. Our estimated shale oil resources in the Rocky Mountains alone are three times the size of Saudi Arabia's oil reserves, which are the world's largest.

We have 27 percent of the world's coal.

As T. Boone Pickens has been pointing out recently, we have huge potential in wind power.

We have enormous opportunities in solar power.

We have the largest number of scientists, engineers, and entrepreneurs of any country in the world.

If we adopt the right strategies and implement sound policies, we can ignore the dictators of the world and never again have to beg another country to help us get energy.

This book, which for the first time synthesizes all my major pro-energy proposals developed in my newsletter *Winning the Future*, my book *Real Change*, and in many other venues, is dedicated to giving you the arguments to win the debate for more American energy now.

ONE

MORE AMERICAN ENERGY NOW

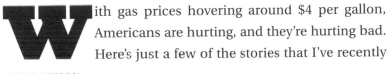ith gas prices hovering around $4 per gallon, Americans are hurting, and they're hurting bad. Here's just a few of the stories that I've recently come across:

- A small appliance repair businessman in Delhi, New York is threatened with going out of business because of the miles he has to log in his car.
- Independent truck drivers in Illinois are working just to cover their costs, one breakdown away from losing their routes.
- A church in Rogers, Arkansas that relies on parishioners' donations has become financially strapped because "all the giving is going in the gas tank."

- Police officers in Tulsa, Oklahoma are forced to patrol their beats on bicycles.
- A "Meals on Wheels" charity in Amarillo, Texas is losing volunteers willing to drive meals to those who need them.
- Families across America are giving up vacations, night school, and even meals because of the high price of gasoline.

The suffering of Americans due to high energy prices is bad enough. But there's more: powerful people believe that Americans–everyday folks just trying to earn a living, feed their families, and help others–are actually the root cause of the energy crisis.

These influential people—many of them the very same individuals who helped create the energy crisis in the first place—have little compassion for the suffering of their fellow countrymen. In fact, they view the energy crisis as just retribution for Americans who, in their minds, have committed the environmental sin of using "too much" energy.

This viewpoint, of course, is woefully misguided. The American people are the chief victims of the energy crisis, not the instigators. To identify those responsible for the current situation, we must look elsewhere.

WHO'S TO BLAME?

The starting point of any discussion of America's energy future has to be this: shortsighted politicians have created the current energy crisis.

For decades anti-energy, left-leaning politicians have advocated higher prices and less energy. Viewing energy usage as a moral failing, they aim to save the environment by punishing Americans into driving less and driving smaller cars. As Speaker Nancy Pelosi has insisted, they're "saving the planet."

Now their policies have been executed with a vengeance. They have stymied almost every major government initiative to expand American energy production, rejecting countless initiatives to increase oil and gas exploration, the extraction of coal, and the development of nuclear power. Now they've finally succeeded in drastically driving up energy prices. And how do they react when Americans begin criticizing the policies that have led to this crisis? They blame "greedy" oil companies, the president, stock speculators—everyone but themselves.

Because they aren't honest about the misguided policies that caused this crisis, these left-leaning politicians can't recommend effective policies that will lead us out of it. They are the problem.

These politicians want scapegoats, while the American people want solutions.

Left-wing politicians cling to a relentlessly anti-oil, anti-coal, anti-nuclear agenda. Their "solution" to the energy crisis is to demand that Americans change their lifestyle to conform to the extremist vision of environmental absolutists. They believe it's wrong for Americans to own big cars or trucks, or to drive long distances for work, vacations, or to visit family. And with sky-high energy prices, more and more Americans can't do these things.

The Left's allergy to oil, coal, and nuclear power is a recipe for continued high energy prices. This affects everyone in the United States who drives a car, uses natural gas to heat their home or cook their meals, or power their lights—in other words, just about every American. And the pain will spread even further in the form of higher inflation as the high cost of energy ripples through the entire economy.

What's more, the negative impact of the Left's polices is not confined to our borders; its platform is also a recipe for making things tougher on the poorest people in developing countries. This is because high energy prices raise the cost of everything from fertilizer to food transportation. In the end, high energy prices are a formula for making the world's hungry even hungrier.

A MATTER OF NATIONAL SECURITY

Not only does the current energy crisis hurt American individuals and weaken the U.S. economy, but it does severe damage to our national security as well. I have been warning for several years that high oil prices on world markets constitute a disastrous setback for America in the war on terror. In July 2006 I wrote:

> Without reduction of energy dependence, America will be subject to the whims of foreign dictators. On July 11, the price of a barrel of crude oil was $74.16. That was the day before Hezbollah kidnapped two Israeli soldiers, which sparked the latest fighting in Lebanon. Three days later, after the fighting began, the price of a barrel of oil was $77.03. That's a $2.87 increase. Now, Iran exports 2.7 million barrels of oil a day. That means if the price of oil stays the same, that $2.87

increase will amount to almost $3 billion more a year for the Iranian dictatorship. That's $3 billion more to spend on rockets for Hezbollah, militias in Iraq and on their nuclear program. Which, by the way, nobody is paying attention to now because of the fighting in Lebanon that Iran almost certainly instigated. So the dictator of Iran is getting the best of both worlds: He gets to attack Israel by funding Hezbollah, and he gets to make all his money back—and then some—from our pocketbooks.

Back then a modest rise in oil prices to $77.03 per barrel was worth $3 billion a year to Iran. The situation has grown much worse since then, with oil prices reaching as high as $147 per barrel—double the price seen just two years ago.

If oil prices stay at their current level, we can estimate that the spike in oil prices will increase Iranian revenues by as much as tens of billions of dollars per year. That is money the mullahs can use to build nuclear weapons and missiles, finance terrorism, and undermine America's allies.

Without drastic action from the United States—the world's largest energy consumer—this state of affairs will only get worse. The worldwide demand for energy will continue to rise, resulting in ever higher energy prices and more money filling the coffers of miscreant oil-producing states. This year, mainland Asia bought more cars than the United States for the first time in history—a sure indication that, unless we act, increasing energy demands from India, China, and others will make affordable energy a thing of the past.

THE SOLUTION: DRILLING
IN AMERICA, FOR AMERICA

There is one solution for reversing this dynamic: increase American energy production. The first steps to expanded production are to change the law to allow more oil and gas development offshore and in Alaska, as well as to lift the prohibition on oil shale development in the West. These measures will drive down today's price for oil and gas by increasing current production, as oil and gas companies try to maximize their profits today before the new oil and gas supplies come online.

With increased American oil production, world oil prices will also be restrained by our declining demand for imported oil. This will curtail the huge influx of money currently pouring into oil producing rogue states like Iran.

Any strategy that does not substantially increase the domestic production of fossil fuels is a strategy for higher prices and growing scarcities. And we certainly have the resources to boost production, since America has the world's largest supply of fossil fuels. We have much more coal than any other country, along with abundant oil and natural gas reserves. The natural resources are there—we just need the government to allow us to extract them.

While it's right to focus on the pain inflicted by the energy crisis, we shouldn't ignore the many opportunities that the crisis presents, especially the opportunity to reduce our debilitating reliance on foreign oil. By drilling for more oil here, in our abundant American reserves, we can produce more affordable energy in America rather than continuing to rely on authoritarian regimes such as those in Saudi Arabia and Venezuela.

We must move away from reliance on foreign oil as soon as possible, especially oil from unstable governments. The current high cost of oil and the instability in the Middle East should help generate the political will and financial incentive to do just that.

DO IT ALL

DO IT NOW

DO IT FOR AMERICA

That should be the theme of our policy geared at steering the billions of dollars per year we spend on foreign oil away from foreign dictators, and toward the expansion of oil production right here at home.

Since this issue impacts both our national security and our economic well-being, we should respond with the intensity and determination with which we've traditionally faced challenges to our national survival.

Increased drilling must be the immediate first step to overcoming the energy crisis. Although we should work toward rapidly expanding alternative energies, we cannot crush Americans during the transition period by doing nothing while their family budgets are exhausted, their jobs are lost, and the price of everything they purchase skyrockets due to the anti-energy elite's refusal to fix the present while waiting around for a better future.

Our elite, anti-oil friends simply do not want to confront the reality that we need more oil now. We need it for the 240 million American cars and trucks that now use gasoline and diesel fuel. We need it for the airline industry, which is being destroyed by the high price of aviation fuel. And we need it to address the reality that for the foreseeable future, the vast majority of cars built throughout the world will rely on oil.

ADDING IN ALTERNATIVE ENERGY

In addition to expanding American oil, coal, and natural gas production, we must move toward a rapid transition to new technologies and new capabilities. We should find alternatives to oil by investing in new technologies to produce safe, clean, reliable, efficient, and inexpensive fuels here at home. This requires a Manhattan Project approach to stimulate advances in biofuels, batteries, hybrid cars, natural gas vehicles, clean coal, liquefied coal, hydrogen, solar, wind, and advanced conservation systems. Such a program should include:

- prizes for specific breakthroughs. Senator John McCain is moving in the right direction when he proposes a $300 million prize for breakthroughs in battery technology that will make electric cars and hybrids work better.
- a bold competition to contract out at least four experimental, next generation clean coal plants to help use coal with virtually no carbon emissions.
- incentives for next generation biofuels, including cellulosic ethanol, that use waste plant material and switchgrass to produce fuel at a competitive price.
- a program for incentivizing energy conservation at every level.

The combination of immediately expanded oil drilling and a long-term program for developing alternative energy forms a strategy that will solve the current energy crisis, while ultimately leading to the availability of unlimited clean energy in a nuclear-hydrogen energy economy. That will give us solutions that can meet increased economic needs while protecting the environment.

CONSERVATION ALONGSIDE PRODUCTION

At the same time we increase production of energy, we must find ways to improve energy conservation. And the path to new breakthroughs in conservation is already being laid out for us.

Contrary to the demonic image of corporate America spread by environmental extremists, it is American companies that are leading the way in innovative techniques for energy conservation.

Experts at Johnson Controls, General Electric, Siemens, Reliant Energy, Honeywell, and elsewhere believe that with a comprehensive approach, energy efficiency could jump as much as 40 percent. Imagine how drastically this could cut energy prices.

Here a few examples of world-class companies making great strides to improve energy efficiency so we can do more with less:

● **General Motors** GM has reduced energy use at its North American facilities by over 27 percent over the last five years and has committed to a 40 percent reduction between 2000 and 2010. The company is also one of the largest corporate users of landfill gas and rooftop solar energy in the United States.

- **Ford Motor Co.** Ford is one of the leading businesses in modeling how the private sector can help solve the energy crisis. Ford has helped reduce energy use by 19 percent for each individual car and has subsequently reduced its total energy use by 30 percent overall. Committed to reducing greenhouse gas emissions, it has set a goal of reducing facility emissions by 10 percent for each vehicle produced between 2002 and 2012.

- **Toyota** Since 2001, Toyota's energy conservation efforts have saved it over $26 million. It's also been setting specific energy saving and performance targets for its future plants. As a result, these performance targets have helped Toyota decrease the intensity of its energy use by 26 percent in eight years.

- **Exxon Mobil** A leader in oil discovery, production, and fuel research, Exxon Mobil has improved its energy efficiency 35 percent over the past twenty-five years, and aims for a further 15 percent improvement in the near future. The company is on the cutting edge of new technologies such as cogeneration, development of the hydrogen vehicle, and carbon capture and storage projects.

These are impressive advances in conservation. However, like our attempts to boost energy production, increasing conservation requires incentives for the entrepreneurial development of new science and technologies.

The government can move conservation forward by approving various tax credits to accelerate maximum efficiency in energy use and to speed up the replacement of outdated systems with more efficient alternatives.

The government could aid conservation by providing these kinds of incentives, but the key is to let consumers choose. The draconian limitations favored by extreme environmentalists and the anti-energy elite are unacceptable and unnecessary. Americans don't want to be told how high or low they're allowed to set their thermostats or what kinds of light bulbs they can or cannot use. The goal is to help the American people—not control them.

YES, WE CAN HAVE IT ALL

The fact is, with leadership that unleashes the potential of the American people, there is no reason why America can't have safe, abundant, and relatively inexpensive energy from a wide range of sources coupled with real breakthroughs in conservation.

Politicians with vision—working with entrepreneurs, scientists, and engineers—could rapidly eliminate the current shortages and bring down prices with a flood of new energy and conservation techniques. America's current vulnerability to blackmail by foreign dictators could be turned into virtual energy independence with a North American energy strategy that includes Canada and Mexico.

The key is to create a new coalition of Americans who favor greater investment, discovery, creativity, conservation, and production. That coalition could lead to a new era of American prosperity with a bigger economy, more abundant energy, healthier environment, and greater national security.

Our elites aren't interested in joining such a coalition. They have reversed Abraham Lincoln's understanding of America.

In a free society governments should serve the people. But the elites' environmental policy is the opposite of Lincoln's call at Gettysburg. It's not government of the people, by the people, for the people; it's government over the people, punishing the people, and telling the people how they can and cannot live their lives.

We have a moral obligation to the American people to make the present prosperous while inventing an even better future. The time has come to re-empower the American people through energy policies designed to create a stronger, technologically advanced economy. The current policies, which serve no end other than limiting the American lifestyle, just won't do.

TWO

THE ARTIFICIAL ENERGY CRISIS

IT DIDN'T HAVE TO HAPPEN

Americans often criticize the government for not having an energy policy. However, America in fact does have an energy policy—it's to make the American people pay outrageous prices for energy.

Our current energy crisis didn't have to happen. It's the result of decades of failed government policies, bureaucratic incompetence, and a system of regulation and litigation that prevents any real development of America's own energy supplies.

To develop a strategy for solving our energy problems, we must first understand how wrongheaded policies brought about our unnecessary crisis.

CONGRESS'S OFFSHORE DRILLING BAN

There is perhaps no better example of the disconnect between your government and you than the ban on offshore oil and gas drilling.

Since 1981, even as the cost of energy has continued to rise, Congress has maintained its ban on any drilling for oil or natural gas in more than 80 percent of all federal waters off our coastlines.[1] Since oil in 1981 was so much cheaper, the Congress at the time didn't believe that cutting off access to America's own energy resources would create any big problems.

As a result of this ban, it is illegal today to drill in the Atlantic, the Pacific, and in the eastern part of the Gulf of Mexico. In most areas, we aren't even allowed to explore just to see how much oil and gas is there.

Instead of the traditional American can-do spirit, Congress's attitude toward drilling can be summed up as "No-We-Can't."

And this attitude still dominates Congress today, despite sky-high oil and gas prices. As Congressman John Boehner put it, this has become a "drill-nothing Congress."

This is no small problem. Every year that this ban remains in place is another year that Americans will needlessly pay high gas prices, with much of the profits going to foreign dictatorships.

CONGRESS'S BAN ON ALASKAN DRILLING

Offshore waters are not the only area where Congress has banned drilling. When the Arctic National Wildlife Refuge (ANWR) was created in 1980, Congress deferred a decision on whether to allow oil drilling there.[2]

As a result, drilling in ANWR is effectively banned until Congress votes to allow it. In 1995, those of us in Congress who wanted to lessen our dependence on foreign oil passed a bill to allow drilling in ANWR only to see it vetoed by President Bill Clinton.

Opponents of ANWR drilling made the same argument in 1995 that they still make today: we wouldn't see a drop of oil for another seven to ten years. Of course, because it's now been thirteen years since President Clinton's veto, we can rightly ask them how much less gas would cost today if they had supported energy independence back then. As Jay Leno joked on the Tonight Show, "At his press conference this week, President Bush blasted Congress for not allowing oil exploration in the Alaskan Wildlife Reserve. Democrats said it wouldn't do any good, because it wouldn't produce oil for ten years. You know—the same thing they said ten years ago."

Unfortunately, Congress continues to oppose lifting the ANWR ban to this day, and Americans continue to pay more at the pump.

CONGRESS'S BAN ON
OIL SHALE DEVELOPMENT

What if someone told you that America has at least three times as much oil as Saudi Arabia—and it's all in the Rocky Mountains?

Would you believe them?

Well, it's true.

The United States has huge amounts of oil shale, which is contained in rock and can be extracted to use in cars and for other purposes.

Unsurprisingly, this is another major source of energy that the anti-energy Congress has put off limits. In June 2007, Colorado Democratic congressman Mark Udall inserted an amendment into a spending bill, approved six months later, that essentially halted any oil shale development until Congress decides to lift the ban.

Clearly, Congress has a different set of priorities from those of the American people. The average anti-energy member of Congress looks at the potential for drilling for oil shale and asks, "How can we stop it?" Meanwhile, Americans are demanding, "Why aren't we drilling now?"

If we want to solve the energy crisis, keeping the biggest U.S. oil deposits off-limits to exploration and production is not a helpful policy. To the contrary, it's a surefire guarantee that we'll never break our dependence on foreign oil.

LAWSUITS THAT PREVENT DRILLING

There is absolutely no doubt that out-of-control litigation has added to the energy crisis.

Environmental extremist organizations routinely file lawsuits to stop drilling even when environmental regulations have been followed to the letter. Their goal is not to ensure that regulations are followed, but rather to stop all drilling—permanently.

And this problem is getting worse. In 2001, 27 percent of all leases issued for drilling in the Rockies were challenged in court. This figure jumped to 81 percent by 2007—a tripling of the ratio of challenges in just six years.

A recent example of litigation choking off American energy supplies was seen in Alaska, where Shell Oil has spent over $200 million buying leases and equipping ships and personnel in the Beaufort Sea. The Minerals Management Service, which oversees offshore drilling regulations, conducted a full environmental study to ensure that Shell's proposed activities there would be environmentally safe. But that wasn't enough for the Center for Biological Diversity (CBD), which challenged the permits for drilling in the Ninth Circuit Court of Appeals, a court well known for its extreme liberal rulings. Unsurprisingly, the court ruled to suspend drilling.[3]

Both the government and Shell have gone to great lengths to protect the environment in this area, but no amount of regulations will ever satisfy anti-energy absolutists. In fact, an attorney for the CBD admitted publicly that the goal of the lawsuit wasn't to force Shell to follow regulations or to stop drilling in that particular location, but rather to stop *all* drilling in Alaska.

Meanwhile, Shell has invested hundreds of millions of dollars in the Beaufort Sea and over $2 billion in buying the right to drill in other areas off the Alaskan coast. If the judgment from this lawsuit stands, Shell will have lost billions of dollars and wasted valuable time and manpower, and America will have lost another source of energy.

Perhaps most important, the case will make all oil companies more reluctant to explore new sources of oil in the United States. After seeing Shell lose its entire project due to a frivolous lawsuit, who would want to risk investing the millions of dollars needed to develop a new field?

The current situation cries out for fundamental litigation reform. Without it, environmental activists and their lawyers will continue to stand in the way of commonsense energy solutions.

REGULATIONS AND BUREAUCRACY
THAT SUFFOCATE OIL DEVELOPMENT

One of the major sources of the energy crisis is the bureaucratic nightmare that energy companies face when they want to drill for oil. A Department of the Interior study found that of the 30.5 billion barrels of oil estimated to be undeveloped on federal lands, fully 62 percent is inaccessible because of regulations and moratoriums.[4]

Needless to say, no country that prohibits the extraction of three-fifths of its undeveloped onshore oil can ever hope to become energy independent.

While some regulations are necessary for environmental protection, many others are just ridiculous. For example, a few years ago in southeastern New Mexico, the Bureau of Land Management (BLM)—which oversees most regulations relating to onshore oil and gas drilling—put a moratorium on drilling in 380,000 acres of land from April through June because it was afraid that drilling might interfere with the mating season of prairie chickens.

Regardless of whether or not it's wise to limit our energy extraction because it might upset a few amorous chickens, the worst part about the moratorium was that it wasn't based on any scientific analysis. When the oil industry demanded that one be conducted, the BLM announced it would consider reducing the moratorium to only 196,000 acres.[5] Undoubtedly, the powerful prairie chicken lobby was furious with the decision.

Another case of harmful energy regulation is evident in the Mongongahela National Forest in West Virginia, where bureaucrats tried to conduct an environmental assessment on drilling.

The rules were written so vaguely and the instructions given by the Forest Service were so conflicting that it took bureaucrats two years and ten drafts before they completed the report. What's especially infuriating is that some of the rejected drafts were exactly the same as earlier versions that had already been rejected.

But why should it come as any surprise that bureaucrats are hindering oil development as they shuffle around the same papers over and over again? They're bureaucrats; that's what they're good at.

If we want to break out of the energy crisis, we'll need to streamline these kinds of regulations, reduce the arbitrary power of bureaucracies to hinder development, and unleash the tremendous power of free enterprise.

REGULATIONS THAT STRANGLE NEW OIL REFINERIES

Any solution to the current energy crisis will have to increase our ability to refine crude oil into usable fuel. The American people understand that we need to produce more American oil by building more refineries, but the combination of bureaucracy, litigation, and bad tax policies have made this almost impossible.

The United States hasn't built a new refinery since 1976. When we don't have enough refineries, we have to import more refined fuel that is more expensive than imported crude oil. If we don't increase our refining capacity, it won't matter how much oil we get from drilling offshore or anywhere else because we won't be able to turn it into high-quality fuel.

Additionally, as a matter of principle, any time U.S. manufacturers can add value to a product it helps keep in America good jobs and income that we would otherwise export.

The current situation is unacceptable. For example, Arizona Clean Fuels has been trying to build a technologically advanced oil refinery in Arizona for years. The company first starting working to get a permit for the refinery in 1998, when it was going to be built in Mobile, Arizona. But in 2003 state regulations prevented the company from building in Mobile, so it moved to a remote site thirty-five miles east of Yuma. It wasn't until 2005 that the permits to build were finally approved—seven years after the process began.[6]

But that wasn't the end of the story. After receiving its permits, the company had to raise enough money to build the estimated $4 billion refinery. This took several years, and then in 2008 the company was forced to move its location yet again, to a site three miles east of the original site, because of a lawsuit by an Indian tribe in California. Finally, after more than a decade, Arizona Clean Fuels is scheduled to begin construction of the refinery in early 2009. But because the project is so massive and complex, it won't be finished until 2012. That means that from start to finish, it will have taken Arizona Clean Fuels about fourteen years to build a new refinery.[7]

Meanwhile, our shortage of refineries is being exploited by other countries, particularly India, which is quickly becoming the world's center for oil refining. In 2007 the Indian government announced it would increase its refining capacity by 62 percent within the next five years. Thus, India plans to raise its entire refining capacity by three-fifths in less time than it took Arizona Clean Fuels to get the permits to build a single refinery.

India's biggest refiner, Reliance Industries, has been leading the way in transforming India into a major oil refiner. Reliance began building its first refinery, which is one-third the size of Manhattan, at Jamnagar in 1996 and finished in thirty-six months. The company decided to expand the site in December 2005 and will finish constructing a new refinery ahead of schedule by the end of 2008. When the new refinery comes online, the Jamnagar site will have a capacity of 1.24 million barrels per day, making it the largest refinery in the world.[8]

Most important, this second, huge refinery is being built exclusively to process oil to export to Europe and the United States. It will be able to process the lowest quality crude oil into the highest-quality, most environmentally safe gasoline available, something only thirty other refineries in the world can do, and none at the capacity of Jamnagar.

If we want to remain competitive in the international economy, we can't simply cede to foreign countries profitable economic activities like oil refining solely because of dysfunctional regulations.

THE BUREAUCRATIC BUNGLING OF CLEAN COAL

The staggering number of regulations that restrict energy exploration and the stifling bureaucracy that implements them hinder more than just oil exploration. There is no better example of this than the Department of Energy's (DOE) "Future Gen" project for clean coal.

In December 2003, DOE announced Future Gen as a plan to build the first clean coal power plant and have it operating in five years.

It took four years before the DOE finally decided where Future Gen would be built. Then, in January 2008, the department claimed it had to restructure the project and construction would no longer begin in 2008 as planned. By May, having abandoned its original plan entirely, the DOE announced Future Gen would not become operational until at least 2016.

Meanwhile, the Chinese in 2005 announced they would build their own version of a clean coal plant called Green Gen that would be operational by 2009.

There is something seriously wrong when the U.S. government bureaucracy takes eleven years to build what it said it could in five and what the Chinese *will* build in four.

Consequently, the first country likely to invent the technology necessary for clean coal plants will be China, not the United States. And the first country to sell that technology to other countries for a profit will also be China. We are falling behind in coal technology because of an incompetent and destructive bureaucracy that threatens to keep energy prices high while lowering the U.S. standard of technological innovation.

RESTRAINTS ON NUCLEAR POWER

Nuclear power is another energy source facing unjustified government restraints. In 1979 there was a panic about nuclear power as a result of the accident at the Three Mile Island nuclear power plant, along with the near-simultaneous release of the anti-nuclear movie "The China Syndrome." In response, U.S. politicians made an emotional, short-sighted decision to approve regulations making it extremely difficult to build nuclear power plants. As a result, we have not licensed a new nuclear power plant in nearly thirty years. In fact, bureaucratic obstacles make it so difficult to construct new plants that the nuclear power industry largely doesn't think it's even worth trying anymore. Strikingly, during roughly this period when no new nuclear power plants were built (1970–2008), electricity prices have *quintupled*.

Between 1979 and 2007, in contrast, Japan constructed thirty-six new nuclear power plants and had eleven more under development, while France built fifty-six plants. And many other countries are now racing to expand nuclear power in order to minimize their carbon dioxide emissions while producing vast quantities of cheap, clean energy.

What's more, experts now consider nuclear power plants as a very safe form of energy. Anti-nuclear activists like to invoke the 1986 Chernobyl meltdown as a symbol of the danger of nuclear power. However, a Soviet-designed nuclear plant built nearly three decades ago is hardly indicative of the safety of today's technologically advanced nuclear plants. Nevertheless, U.S. bureaucrats and politicians continue to resist the expansion of nuclear power, depriving Americans of yet another efficient source of energy.

The next time you find yourself being lectured by liberals about the dangers of carbon dioxide emissions and global warming, remind your left-leaning friends that if the United States got 75 percent of its electricity from nuclear power, as France does, there would be 2.2 billion fewer tons of carbon dioxide in the atmosphere each year. Then ask why *they're* unwilling to help fight global warming by supporting nuclear power.

OBSTACLES TO WIND AND
SOLAR TECHNOLOGY

Congress claims to champion alternative energy, but it even discourages clean, renewable energy solutions such as wind and solar power. The best tool for encouraging the use of these energies is the tax credits passed as part of the 2005 Energy Policy Act. However, these tax credits, which make wind and solar power more affordable and competitive with other energy forms, will expire at the end of 2008 unless renewed by Congress.

But even their renewal will not be enough. By refusing to make these tax credits permanent, Congress has made it impossible for wind and solar industries to plan for the future. Businesses just don't want to risk investing a lot of money now to develop some new technology if they suspect their tax credits might expire a few years down the road.

And the problem isn't just with Congress—bureaucrats and regulations are also stopping us from developing solar technology. For example, in May 2008 the Bureau of Land Management announced it would stop accepting new applications for solar energy development projects in the six western states that provide the best locations for these projects. The bureau wanted the moratorium in order to conduct a two-year long assessment of how these projects would affect the environment.[9]

This would have throttled the solar industry in its infancy just as it's starting to take off. And the moratorium wasn't even necessary—the BLM could have continued to accept applications while studying the environmental impact at the same time.

Eventually, it was forced to do just that in response to outrage from the solar industry and the public.

UNDERSTANDING THE "NO-WE-CAN'T" MINDSET

Our energy crisis could have been avoided if anti-energy elitists had simply allowed the development of more American energy to increase supply and lower prices.

The price of gas is causing real financial hardship to American workers and families. One economist calculated that the price of oil rising from $80 per barrel to $100 had the same effect on Americans' wallets as a $150 billion tax increase.

So how is it that the anti-energy elitists in Congress continually refuse to lessen this burden? The answer boils down to a question of values.

"No-We-Can't" liberals say no to drilling, no to oil shale, no to clean coal, and no to nuclear power, while saying yes to taxes, litigation, and regulation. What explains these policies, which all result in higher prices and less energy?

Clearly, these politicians value something else above the interests of everyday Americans. Leaders who care first and foremost about the needs of Americans will try to ensure that American families don't have to choose between buying clothes and buying gasoline. They'll seek to protect small businesses from going under due to high energy costs, and they'll try to keep companies from having to lay off their workers for the same reason. They'll want to make sure that the economy functions so that our money stays in America to develop American jobs and protect our national security.

They'll want to do all of this while protecting the environment—but they'll always remember that the people come first.

Anti-energy absolutists, however, object to any energy development that would affect the environment in almost any way, regardless of the cost to the American people. They adhere to a romantic vision of a "pure" environment unspoiled by human activity, and they seek to regulate the minutest areas of our lives—from the cars we drive to our house thermostats—in order to preserve that utopian vision.

That's why the anti-energy elites constantly declare that the American people need to "sacrifice" to solve the energy crisis. They call on Americans to eat less meat, do laundry less often, wash dishes by hand, and vacation closer to home.

This is the same type of restrictive, government-controlled energy policy that former President Jimmy Carter supported in the 1970s. Back then, he warned Americans that solving our energy problems "will demand that we make sacrifices and changes in our lives. To some degree, the sacrifices will be painful—but so is any meaningful sacrifice. It will lead to some higher costs, and to some greater inconveniences for everyone."

Some of us are old enough to remember the result of President Carter's policies: shortages, rationing, overbearing bureaucracy—and repudiation at the polls by the American people in 1980.

Unfortunately, even Democratic presidential candidate Barack Obama shares the anti-energy mentality. During his campaign, he let Americans know how terrible our way of life is: "We can't drive our SUVs and, you know, eat as much as we want and keep our homes on, you know, 72 degrees at all times, and whether we're living in the desert or we're living in the tundra, and then just expect that every other country's going to say okay."

We may hear from our doctors that we can't eat as much as we want, but it sounds eerie coming from a politician. Is the "No-We-Can't" Left planning to ban the buffet line as well?

This points to the real agenda behind much of the extreme environmental movement today: an elite group wants to control the way people live, and they aim to do it by controlling people's access to energy. Their policies are specifically designed to keep energy supplies limited, because this scarcity gives them an excuse to enact all sorts of regulations to force people to live in a certain kind of way—a way the elites believe to be environmentally virtuous. It doesn't matter whether or not the people want to live this kind of lifestyle because for the extremists, the environment comes first, the people second.

The choice is between allowing Americans to live the lives of prosperity and happiness that they have become used to, or forcing them to radically change their lifestyles by punishing them with taxes and regulation.

The vast majority of the American people favor more energy, lower prices, and prosperous lives. But anti-energy elites view the American way of life as greedy, wasteful, and immoral. For them, expensive energy provides a way to impose their personal lifestyle choices on the rest of us.

THE FAILURE OF
ENVIRONMENTAL EXTREMISM

Not only is the anti-energy elitist mentality totally disconnected from the everyday lives of the American people, but it's also detached from the practical realities of how the world works.

Anyone who thinks that a system of more regulation and higher energy taxes will solve our energy crisis is fooling himself. The kinds of international treaties and national energy policies that the elite favor, in fact, will only result in a weaker, poorer, energy-starved America while actually making the global environment worse.

A lot of the restrictions on energy usage favored by environmental extremists are justified as measures to help fight climate change. The problem is that climate change is an international challenge that requires cooperation among all nations. America's unilateral adoption of climate change policies that restrict energy development won't do much to address climate change unless many other countries undertake similar measures.

Above all else, this means that any solutions we adopt in order to deal with climate change must also be adopted by China and India. In 2007, China overtook the United States as the leading emitter of carbon dioxide, with India coming in third. The United Nations Development Program has stated, rightly, that no climate change agreement has any chance of success without the inclusion of these two countries, as well as numerous poor, developing nations.

But both China and India have already made clear that they won't adopt climate change policies that hurt their economies. Both nations strenuously oppose carbon-capping systems such as the Kyoto Protocol, which would surely interfere with their current breakneck pace of economic growth.

To truly address concern about climate change we need solutions that China and India will adopt voluntarily, which means the policies have to benefit their economies instead of harming them. Such solutions should encourage the development of new technologies that pollute less, are more efficient, and cost about the same as current technologies. For example, the invention of an affordable emissions-free car would dramatically reduce carbon emissions, and it would be acceptable to China and India because their people would willingly buy it.

Pragmatically, the only way to address concerns about climate change is by developing new technologies that will also benefit China and India. If we adopt global warming policies that these nations refuse, we'll simply be hindering our own economy without making any meaningful impact on climate change.

EXPORTING OUR JOBS AND FACTORIES WON'T HELP THE ENVIRONMENT

A few years ago, Belgium adopted a carbon cap-and-trade system, which places an overall cap on businesses' carbon emissions. A large cement factory there lost so much money due to the new regulations and penalties that its owners closed it down and relocated to Morocco, where they could make a lot more money because Morocco didn't have a cap-and-trade system. So, Belgium lost jobs, Morocco gained jobs, and the cement factory produced even more carbon and pollution under Morocco's lax regulations than it had been producing in Belgium before the cap and trade system began. From both an economic and an environmental standpoint, the cap-and-trade system was a total failure.

This example demonstrates one of the biggest flaws in the elitist mentality toward energy and climate change: the assumption that jobs and businesses have to stay in the United States.

They don't.

And they won't under an anti-energy, anti-business system of regulation and taxation. Businesses will go where they can make the most money at the lowest cost. If faced with a system that makes energy more expensive and limits how much they can produce, businesses will simply pack up and move somewhere with less strict regulations. The result will be fewer American jobs, while global warming and air pollution will actually grow worse.

The American chemical industry has been particularly hard hit by rising American energy prices, with every $1 increase in the price for a barrel of oil costing the industry $660 million. And the rise in natural gas prices is even more damaging, with every $1 per million BTU increase resulting in an additional $3.4 billion cost to the industry.[10]

Rising prices for energy, especially natural gas, have cost the chemical industry over 100,000 jobs over the last decade. The consequences of this have been dire for most American manufacturers. Over 96 percent of all manufactured goods are directly touched by chemistry, and industries that rely upon chemistry generate one-fifth of U.S. GDP. Notably, chemical industry products such as insulation also help improve the nation's overall energy efficiency. The difficulties facing U.S. manufacturers have resulted in significant job losses, with some companies forced to relocate overseas.

Natural gas markets are localized, meaning that prices in North America only affect North American producers. Increased exploration and development of American natural gas resources would thus quickly lower energy costs and offer some immediate relief to American manufacturers.

We have to remember that most countries don't care about the environment nearly as much as the United States does. For example, in 2006 China, India, and the United States all built new coal-fired power plants, which emit large amounts of carbon into the air. However, China built so many plants that they were bringing online more electric power from coal each week than the United States and India combined over the course of the year. This is representative of China's explosive economic growth rate, which it will maintain regardless of the environmental consequences. And of course, every U.S. business that moves to China to avoid our regulations and taxation will likely become a much worse polluter than they ever had been in the United States.

Just look at the oil fields, for example, in Russia, Nigeria, Kuwait, Saudi Arabia, Indonesia, and many other big oil-producing states, where environmental standards are not nearly as strict as they are in the United States. Those environmental extremists who stridently oppose domestic oil production don't seem to mind the serious environmental damage done by the countries that export oil to us. By preventing us from drilling for more oil in

America, where drilling is more environmentally sensitive than anywhere else, these extremists are effectively condoning environmental degradation in other nations that are out of sight, out of mind.

The bottom line is this: high taxes and burdensome regulations chase away American businesses, and the businesses take their jobs with them—usually to countries that don't particularly care about the environment. Cap-and-trade proposals like the Boxer-Warner-Lieberman bill that was introduced in 2008 should really be called the "China Full Employment Act" because they will result in a dramatic exodus of U.S. companies to foreign countries.

Today, the United States is locked in fierce economic competition with nations such as China, South Korea, Japan, and India. We cannot pretend that adopting restrictive environmental policies won't affect our ability to compete with these countries for jobs and businesses. If we chase out our own businesses in the name of environmental extremism, we'll be doomed to a future of slow economic growth in which Asian nations become the leading industrialized countries in the world. We must recognize instead that in order to compete in the global economy, we need to reform our policies to be more efficient and more technologically advanced. We need to compete through innovation and entrepreneurs, not regulation and bureaucrats.

But if we continue down the current road of high taxation and strict regulation, we'll ensure high energy prices, limited economic growth, and ultimately, we'll concede our economic leadership to China and other nations.

CAP-AND-TRADE WILL
INCREASE CORRUPTION

A tax-and-regulate system (a more accurate way to describe "cap-and-trade") is based on the absurd idea that Congress will be able to impose limits on pollution equally and fairly without being influenced by lobbyists and special interest groups.

But every time a new bill for more taxation and regulation comes before Congress, there is a longer line of lobbyists seeking special favors in whatever new system is created.

The moment a cap-and-trade or some similar system is put in place (if not before), big corporations and other rich businesses will send in swat teams of lobbyists to convince Congress to exempt their particular business from any given regulation or tax. They'll be relentless because they'll know how much money is riding on their ability to shape the new system to their own advantage. So the burden of the new regulations and taxes will fall squarely on the millions of small businesses and local corporations that don't have the resources to influence Congress. The result will be a profoundly unfair system in which the rich and powerful get off easy and small business owners get crushed.

This is not just some theory—it already happened when the European Union adopted its cap-and-trade system. When European governments were deciding how to limit carbon emissions, there was such intense lobbying from big, well-connected businesses that the emissions cap ended up being higher than the actual emissions.

So the system didn't actually reduce carbon emissions, but it did allow major corporations to make big money by fixing the rules in their favor. Meanwhile, small factories and businesses have struggled under the new rules in which they had no say.

WHAT THE AMERICAN PEOPLE REALLY WANT

As usual, the American people understand the energy crisis and the kind of commonsense strategies needed to solve it better than the out-of-touch Washington bureaucracy. While politicians and bureaucrats blame each other—or the American people—for the problem, Americans are speaking with one voice about a solution: more American energy now!

Americans have one immediate priority when it comes to energy: lower prices. By a 71-18 percent margin, people want Congress to focus on "increasing the energy supplies of the United States and lowering the costs of gasoline and electricity," according to a poll conducted by American Solutions, a non-partisan, grassroots advocacy organization that I serve as chairman.[11] From listening to the media and Washington politicians, however, you would think that the issue of increased drilling for oil was another divisive political fight, with Democrats and Republicans lining up on opposite sides.

It's not. Polling data show that expanded energy production, including drilling for more oil and gas off our coasts and in Alaska, is an issue that enjoys not bipartisan, but tripartisan support—a majority of Republicans, independents, and Democrats all support drilling for more American oil. A FoxNews/Opinion Dynamics poll from late July 2008 found that 75 percent of Americans support "increasing drilling for oil in the United States immediately," while only 20 percent opposed it. The policy was favored by

88 percent of Republicans, 77 percent of independents, and 66 percent of Democrats.

That's right—two-thirds of Democratic voters support drilling for more oil right now. In fighting tooth and nail against drilling, Democratic leaders in Washington are ignoring the voices of their own rank-and-file members.

The level of support is nearly identical for offshore drilling, which environmental extremists and their allies in Congress have resisted for decades. Polls show 71 percent of Americans support drilling more "in U.S. coastal areas," with only 23 percent opposed.

Even in the most controversial drilling site, Alaska's Arctic National Wildlife Refuge (ANWR), more and more people are demanding development of oil resources. Fifty-six percent of Americans now want Congress to allow drilling in ANWR, including a majority of independents and 45 percent of Democrats. A Zogby poll from June 2008 showed support for drilling in ANWR even higher, at 59 percent. On every issue related to oil and gas production, everyday citizens are united in favor of drilling more and drilling now.

Unlike Washington politicians who believe we must choose between increasing energy production and preserving the environment, Americans realize we can drill for oil in an environmentally responsible way. Seventy-three percent of Americans believe we can have both a strong, energy-rich economy and a healthy environment, another tripartisan majority.

Unsurprisingly, Americans also support greater national investments in clean coal, nuclear, wind, hydrogen, and solar power. Our American Solutions polling shows that 65 percent of Americans support building more nuclear power plants to cut carbon emissions, with only 28 percent opposed. They are even more enthusiastic about clean coal technology, with 71 percent of the people in support of building clean coal plants.

Finally, an overwhelming 81 percent of Americans want to increase funding for research on wind, solar, and hydrogen technologies. These numbers are just the latest example of how optimistic and pragmatic Americans are. Unlike their leaders in Congress, the people know we can solve the energy crisis without harming the environment. They realize the necessity of increased drilling, as well as the enormous potential for alternative energy sources to provide us with greater amounts of clean energy over time to allow our economy to grow.

Compare the approach advocated by the American people—expanded drilling, clean coal, nuclear power, and alternative energy sources—with that of the liberal, environmental elite. As we have seen, the elite oppose the first three steps, and have even done serious damage to the wind and solar industries.

Instead of focusing on lowering energy costs by increasing energy supplies as the vast majority of Americans clearly want, anti-energy elitists have focused on raising federal taxes on gasoline in order to cut carbon emissions.

Unfortunately, these same people largely control both Congress and the media, and their disconnect from the realities of everyday life in America prevents them from understanding the immediate priorities of the American people.

Even many supporters of cap-and-trade acknowledge that such a system would increase the cost of gasoline and electricity. When Americans are asked how much more money they are willing to pay at the pump due to the imposition of cap-and-trade, 65 percent say they wouldn't pay a dime more. When the same question is asked about paying more for electricity, that number rises to 71 percent.

Another major proposal commonly heard from anti-energy elitists is to increase the gasoline tax in order to force Americans to use less oil. Although it's hard to believe any politician could be so out of touch as to seek to raise the gas tax at a time when gas prices are near all-time highs, the idea is still popular in some elite circles.

Hiking the gas tax is not supported by the American people, however. A FoxNews poll found that 82 percent of the people oppose increasing the gas tax—another tripartisan majority, and one that includes 79 percent of Democrats.

Americans have made their position clear: they want to reduce carbon emissions, but not in a way that raises energy prices or prevents the development of more energy sources.

"THE UNNECESSARY CRISIS": A LESSON FROM WINSTON CHURCHILL

In his memoirs, former British prime minister Winston Churchill wrote about a discussion he had with Franklin Roosevelt about World War II: "One day President Roosevelt told me that he was asking publicly for suggestions about what the war should be called. I said at once, 'The Unnecessary War.' There never was a war more easy to stop than that which has just wrecked what was left of the world from the previous struggle."

Nothing could be more accurate in describing our current energy crisis than to say it was unnecessary—Washington politicians and bureaucrats have ignored warnings of an impending energy crisis for years.

Anti-energy elitists have said no to drilling, no to coal, no to nuclear power, and no to oil shale. At the same time, they have supported more taxation, regulation, and litigation. This uniquely destructive combination of policies has led us into the current crisis. But just as this nation summoned all its courage, willpower, and resources to win World War II, we can marshal the same commitment to end our energy crisis and lower prices right now. All we have to do is unleash the resources we already have right here in America. In the next chapter, we'll discuss how America can wake up and become an energy giant.

THREE

WE HAVE THE POWER

WHY AMERICA SHOULD BE AN ENERGY POWERHOUSE

This chapter will explain something that some people don't want you to know: when it comes to energy resources, America is a sleeping giant, with potentially the largest energy reserves of any country in the world. Although decades of ever-increasing anti-energy regulations have crippled our ability to produce energy, with the right policies America could rival—and even exceed—the world's biggest energy powerhouses.

Here are a few facts to consider:

- We have an estimated 31 billion barrels of oil and 231 trillion cubic feet of natural gas located onshore, and we'll probably find much more if we're allowed to explore.

- We have an estimated 86 billion barrels of oil and 420 trillion cubic feet of natural gas lying undeveloped offshore.

- We have three times as much oil as Saudi Arabia in estimated oil shale deposits located in just the three states of Colorado, Utah, and Wyoming.

- We could dramatically lower the cost of electricity by developing a technologically advanced, safe, and emission-free nuclear power industry like the ones that France and even the "green" state of Vermont have.

- We have enormous potential for wind energy, while solar power technology is rapidly advancing from California to Florida.

- Auto manufacturers and other scientists here in America are developing hydrogen-powered fuel cells and advanced batteries that could fundamentally transform the basic energy used to transport people and goods.

- We have the most innovative, resourceful, and entrepreneurial population in the world, one that can accomplish undreamed of breakthroughs in technology that will change the way we live, end our energy crisis, and better protect the environment.

And that's just the beginning. As you'll see in this chapter, we're not running out of energy. In fact, America possesses natural resources on a scale that is truly spectacular.

OIL AND NATURAL GAS ONSHORE AND
IN THE OUTER CONTINENTAL SHELF

Anti-energy elites frequently argue that we don't have enough oil in the United States to reduce substantially the amount that we import. Don't believe them. We have huge amounts of oil, we have the technology to access it safely, and unbelievably, the only thing stopping us is our own government.

The Bureau of Land Management estimated in 2008 that we have 31 billion barrels of oil and 231 trillion cubic feet of natural gas located on 279 million acres of federal lands.[1] These are incredible numbers. Consider this: if we produce just 1 million more barrels of oil a day, it would reduce our dependence on foreign dictators by 7.5 percent and increase total American production by almost 20 percent.

Right now, by law, we can only explore for energy on 15 percent of mainland America's Outer Continental Shelf (OCS), the area off our coasts. That small amount of offshore drilling accounts for 25 percent of our oil production. Opening up the other 85 percent of the OCS would make vastly more oil available to Americans. The Minerals Management Service, which oversees our resources offshore, estimates that we have 86 billion barrels of undiscovered recoverable oil and 420 trillion cubic feet of undiscovered recoverable natural gas offshore. This is in addition to the 15.4 billion barrels of oil and 60.2 trillion cubic feet of gas we already know exist offshore.[2]

Since we consume about 7 billion barrels of oil each year (two-thirds of which is imported from abroad), we have enough oil offshore alone to cover our oil needs for over a decade. But because we can't produce or refine the oil that quickly, it would last much longer. Although it would not eradicate our dependence on foreign oil, it would dramatically reduce it and lower prices at the pump.

OFFSHORE ENERGY RESOURCES [OCS]

■ OFF-LIMITS TO ENERGY EXPLORATION
■ ONLY AVAILABLE OFFSHORE AREA OPEN TO EXPLORATION IN THE CONTINENTAL UNITED STATES

OFF-LIMITS OIL SHALE **800** BILLION BARRELS

OFF-LIMITS

OFF-LIMITS

OPEN

ONLY 3% OF OFFSHORE GOV'T LAND IS CURRENTLY LEASED FOR ENERGY EXPLORATION.

SOURCE: http://www.instituteforenergyresearch.org/images/OCS_Map.jpg

I≡R INSTITUTE FOR ENERGY RESEARCH

OIL IN ALASKA AND THE ARCTIC CIRCLE

The Arctic National Wildlife Refuge (ANWR) is the best example of the incredible energy resources we have onshore in this country. While the entire refuge is 19 million acres large, roughly the size of South Carolina, the government's best estimate is that 10.4 billion barrels of recoverable oil are located under just 1.5 million acres in a flat, northern area called the "coastal plain" or "10-02 area." This is an astounding amount of oil potentially located on an amazingly small patch of land. For some perspective, that is twice as much oil as Texas has in proven reserves.

And we wouldn't even need to drill that entire parcel to recover all that oil. By using the latest drilling technology, it's estimated that only 2,000 acres of the coastal plain would actually be affected. That means that overall, drilling would affect just one ten-thousandth of ANWR's land. As Frank Luntz said, "If ANWR was the *New York Times*, the area in question is the size of a single letter on the page."

As we've seen, a large majority of Americans support drilling in ANWR, which can be done without damaging the coastal plain or otherwise harming the environment. What's more, over 75 percent of Alaskans, including residents of the only village located inside ANWR, support drilling in the reserve. This should come as no surprise, since ANWR drilling would create and sustain up to 130,000 jobs in Alaska and elsewhere, according to the Bureau for Labor Statistics. So Congress's ban on ANWR drilling not only costs us at the pump, but it costs American jobs as well.

Drilling in ANWR would also provide a giant stream of new revenues for the government without raising taxes. The Congressional Research Service estimated that the taxes and royalties from ANWR's 10.4 billion barrels of oil would total $191 billion.[3] It also means the U.S. would spend over $1.3 trillion here at home for oil, rather than sending that money to foreign countries.

And ANWR is not the only potential source of oil around Alaska. In fact, the U.S. Geological Survey reports there is even more oil, as well as giant reserves of natural gas, located offshore.

When you think of drilling for oil, you probably think of oil rigs in the balmy Gulf of Mexico or on the plains of sunny Texas. But imagine an oil rig surrounded by miles-long icebergs near the frigid Arctic Circle. Thanks to the amazing advances in technology achieved over the last few decades, energy companies can now drill in the seas off of Alaska and north of the Arctic Circle, areas that contain huge amounts of oil and natural gas.

The U.S. Geologic Survey estimated in July 2008 that there are as many as 90 billion barrels of oil and 1.8 quadrillion cubic feet of natural gas north of the Arctic Circle. At least 30 billion of those barrels of oil are thought to be within U.S. boundaries. These estimates add to the 40 billion barrels of oil and 1.1 quadrillion cubic feet of natural gas that have already been discovered in that area.[4] They would be worth over $760 billion in taxes and royalties and $5.2 trillion to the U.S. economy.

Drilling off the Alaskan coast would unlock a truly vast amount of energy. But this is all lost to us until we fundamentally change our energy policy. And while we dawdle, others are hard at work exploring and staking claims in the Arctic. These include among others the Danes, Canadians, and Russians, all of whom believe that the current estimates of energy resources in that region are very conservative.

UNDERESTIMATING OUR ENERGY POTENTIAL

Recall how much oil and natural gas you've just read is available in the United States.

Now double it. And there might be even more than that.

The fact is, the figures I've provided probably underestimate how much oil and gas we really have. Estimating the size of an oil or gas field before drilling is a difficult science involving many complex factors. Once production begins, analysts often find that the field can produce vastly more oil and gas than they originally expected. This increase in oil and gas reserves over time from existing wells is known as "reserve growth."

Here are just a few examples:

- In 1984, the Gulf of Mexico was estimated by the Minerals Management Service to hold 6 billion barrels of oil and 60 trillion cubic feet of natural gas. Since that time, companies have actually produced 13 billion barrels of oil and 152 trillion cubic feet of natural gas, more than doubling the initial estimates. This is in part because the government in 1995 changed laws to encourage investment in the very deep waters off the Gulf, which many had written off as an area that had been drained dry. Companies poured billions into new technology and created new jobs, revenues, and energy.

- In 1977, when oil production first began at Prudhoe Bay on Alaska's North Slope, the reserve estimate there was 9 billion barrels. Since then, because of more discoveries and better technology, over 15 billion barrels have been produced and shipped from the area—a 66 percent increase over the initial estimates.

- Following the 2007 discovery of the Tupi Field off the coast of Brazil, experts initially estimated that the field contained 5-10 billion barrels of commercially recoverable oil. However, once oil companies began drilling, estimates tripled to 30 billion barrels. Until the 2007 discovery, Brazil's future oil production looked dim. That's not the case anymore.

- In 2008, analysts increased their estimate of Italy's Ombrina Mare reserves by 400 percent to 20 million barrels.

- In 1995 the U.S. Geological Survey estimated that the Bakken Formation, located in parts of the Dakotas and Montana, could hold 151 million barrels of oil. But in

April 2008 it increased its top estimate by 2,000 percent to 3 billion barrels of oil.

In addition to reserve growth from existing wells, you must remember there are still vast areas of land that we haven't yet explored. Alaska in particular holds great promise for having
drastically higher oil reserves than currently known. Although
twice the size of Texas, the state has just 1,644 producing oil wells,
compared to 144,660 wells in the Lone Star State. Even relatively
tiny West Virginia, with 3,408 wells, more than doubles Alaska's
well count. Generally speaking, Alaska remains untapped, as does
federal land in most western states.

So keep this in mind—the United States may have dramatically
more oil and natural gas resources than we even know. But we
will never find out if we can't or won't look. We should recall that
before oil was discovered in Prudhoe Bay in 1968, dozens of wells
had been drilled all over Alaska's North Slope to no avail. Atlantic
Richfield Corporation was drilling its last approved well when it
hit the largest field ever discovered in North America.

That's why Senator Barack Obama's proposal (Senate Bill 115)
to repeal a law requiring inventories of American deepwater energy resources every five years is so troubling. How can we increase our energy supply if we're prevented from discovering
where our energy resources are hidden?

OIL SHALE

Locked away in regions of Colorado, Wyoming, and Utah are the
largest deposits of oil shale in the world. Oil shale is a type of rock

that releases kerogen, a paraffin or wax-like substance, when it's heated. To get the oil from the rock, we have to heat it and then capture the oil that's released. This process is called retorting.

Oil shale represents one of America's most incredible potential sources of energy. One estimate from a 2005 study requested by the Department of Energy found that the Green River Formation—which is spread out over Colorado, Wyoming, and Utah—may hold up to 1 trillion barrels of recoverable oil. Even the more likely estimate of 800 billion barrels is over three times the amount of the proven oil reserves in Saudi Arabia.

The traditional challenge of obtaining oil from shale is that the process is expensive, potentially harmful to the environment, and uses large amounts of water. But new technologies being developed have made oil shale much more cost effective and environmentally sound. Shell Oil has already tested a new in-situ (on site) method of extraction that involves placing heating rods into the ground and then collecting the liquid in a pool below. Initial estimates suggest that this process, which would dramatically lessen the environmental impact of oil shale development, could be profitable if a barrel of oil were as cheap as $25.

Thanks to constantly evolving technology, the possibilities for developing oil shale have never been brighter. But we must be allowed to try.

METHANE HYDRATES

Even though you probably haven't heard of them, methane hydrates could be a key solution to our energy challenges. Methane hydrates is a technical term for frozen natural gas found on the

ocean floor and in permafrost around the Arctic. The U.S. Geological Society (USGS) estimates that the earth's ice holds up to
300 million trillion cubic feet of natural gas.

It's difficult to even comprehend how much energy that is, so
here are a few numbers to put it in context. USGS believes there
are 13,000 trillion cubic feet of natural gas left on earth in non-
hydrate form, which is the typical kind of natural gas that we use.
That is the equivalent of 2.2 trillion barrels of oil. The Department
of Energy looked at the amount of methane hydrates to see what
its equivalent would be. Their number: 137.5 trillion barrels of oil.
When you consider the fact that the world has used slightly more
than 1 trillion barrels of oil over the last 150 years, you realize how
staggeringly large these numbers are.

This is a natural resource with amazing potential. It's the world's
largest source of potential fossil energy, and is bigger than all the
coal, oil, oil shale, natural gas, and oil sand resources in the world
combined. The U.S. has 320,000 trillion cubic feet of natural gas
potential in methane hydrates off our coasts. If we could tap into
just 1 percent of that energy we would have enough to supply
America's natural gas needs for 142 years by 2001 standards.

Of course, as with all new sources of energy, there are significant challenges that have to be overcome before we can start
using methane hydrates commercially. We haven't figured out the
most efficient method to extract them yet, and we don't know
what's the best way to protect the environment while doing so.
There is also the question of how using this much natural gas
would affect the global climate, although new research suggests
we might be able to pump carbon dioxide into the ice to help extract the methane and at the same time remove carbon from the

atmosphere. But with such an enormous potential energy source, and one that could use our existing pipe infrastructure, there is no reason for us not to encourage research into making methane hydrates a reality.

NUCLEAR POWER

The potential for nuclear power in this country is tremendous. Today, 104 nuclear power plants operate safely and cleanly in the United States, generating about 20 percent of the nation's electricity without emitting any pollution or carbon dioxide.[5] Unfortunately, we haven't built a new nuclear power plant since the 1970s, and our failure to expand nuclear power has ruined our ability to create a rational energy policy. The Nuclear Energy Institute estimates that to meet the projected increase in U.S. electricity demand by the year 2030, at least thirty-five new nuclear plants will be needed just to maintain nuclear power's current share of total U.S. electricity production.

It's hard to overestimate how important nuclear power is to solving not just our energy crisis, but also our environmental challenges. Nuclear power is emission free and capable of operating twenty-four hours a day. Wind and solar also produce clean power, but they can't supply a constant stream of energy, since the wind is not always blowing and the sun is not always shining.

Not only is nuclear power environmentally safe, but it's also cheaper than the fuels we now use to supply most of our electricity. Nuclear power is nearly six times cheaper than petroleum and nearly four times cheaper than natural gas. Even coal—which produces half our electricity and costs only two-and-a-half cents per kilowatt hour—is more expensive than nuclear power, which costs less than two cents per kilowatt hour.[6] The economic and environmental advantages of nuclear power are simply undeniable.

Equally important, nuclear power has an excellent safety record, contrary to the image put forward by anti-nuclear fringe groups. Nuclear reactors are closely monitored by the Nuclear Regulatory Commission to guarantee that all operations meet the highest standards of safety. That's why from 2000 to 2007 the average accident rate for workers was miniscule—less than 0.2 accidents per 200,000 workers.[7]

Nuclear plant workers do not face an elevated risk of dying from cancer, according to the National Cancer Institute. In fact, a plant worker is exposed to only one-tenth the amount of radiation that an airline pilot who flies from New York to Tokyo is exposed to annually. If you live near a reactor, only about 1 percent of your total exposure to radiation comes from the plant itself.[8]

As previously noted, there has been a deliberate exaggeration of the safety risks of nuclear power plants since the Three Mile Island accident in 1979. But that accident didn't cause even a single death or injury. The melted fuel rods stayed within the reactor, there was no groundwater contamination, and the plant did not release dangerous amounts of radioactive material, as many feared. In fact, the puff of smoke it did emit contained about as much radiation as a single chest X-ray.[9] The other reactor at Three Mile Island has operated without incident since it was reopened in 1985.[10]

The future of nuclear power is indeed bright. In 2001, a group of nations formed the Generation IV International Forum (GIF) to develop the next generation of nuclear power plants. These plants, still in the research and development stage and known as

Generation IV, will have greater safety mechanisms, cost less to construct and operate, and more efficiently dispose of waste material. Right now GIF, which includes the United States, estimates that Generation IV plants will be ready by 2030.[11] But if we make real changes to the suffocating bureaucracy and tax system in this country, it's possible this technology can be ready faster and become a much greater source of clean energy for Americans. The end result will be more power at lower prices, with a cleaner environment to boot.

CLEAN COAL

The United States has been called the "Saudi Arabia of coal." While most of us wouldn't want America to be compared to Saudi Arabia in almost any category, it's absolutely true that our coal reserves are the envy of the world.

Coal currently supplies over half of America's electricity, mostly because it's cheap and abundant.[12] America has the most coal in the world, with 1.5 times as much as Russia, which has the second largest coal reserves, and twice as much as China. In fact, we have even more coal than we do oil and natural gas (which, as you now know, we have aplenty). America holds roughly 27 percent of the world's coal reserves, enough to last another 200–250 years. This is an enormous amount of energy that we have to exploit in order to solve our energy crisis.[13] And these numbers do not even count Alaska's coal resources, which may be larger than those of the entire lower forty-eight states combined.

Our coal reserves provide us with a tremendous opportunity that most countries could only envy. If we use our coal in a smart, environmentally-conscious way, we can dramatically increase our capacity for producing electricity cheaply.

The only thing holding us back is our own broken energy policy. If America committed to developing clean coal technology, we could expand our use of coal at an astounding rate. Because coal is so abundant in America, clean coal technology would provide us with an inexpensive source of power that would provide jobs and cut the cost of electricity for all Americans. We could even turn it into natural gas and convert that to liquid fuels, which would help reduce our dependence on foreign oil. South Africa has been doing that for decades.

And there's no reason why we can't dramatically increase our use of coal while still protecting the environment. We have made tremendous strides in developing carbon capture and storage technology that will soon allow us to use all the coal we need with virtually no carbon emissions. With carbon capture and storage, we prevent the carbon released by a coal plant from going into the atmosphere, instead trapping it and pumping it back underground. The United Nations has estimated that many of these formations would hold carbon emissions safely underground for hundreds of years with virtually none of it escaping into the atmosphere. Some formations could even hold the carbon for millions of years. We don't have to have an America where coal power creates black smokestacks and blankets major cities with soot. With clean coal, we get the benefits of the resource without the traditional dirty side effects of decades past.

We have the coal resources to solve our energy crisis and are developing the technology to use it cleanly. But it will require real change in our energy policies to get there.

WIND POWER

America should be leading the world in wind power generation. One study from Stanford University determined that North America has the greatest wind power potential on earth because of the powerful breezes in the Great Lakes region and along the coasts.[14] This is energy that is renewable, clean, and has no carbon emissions.

It's estimated that wind power could produce twice as much electricity as is used in America today, yet we get much less than 1 percent of our power from wind. By the end of 2008, it's expected that wind will generate enough electricity to power 4.8 million homes, but that's not nearly enough. We need a real push to increase our use of wind and unleash the power of American wind reserves.

T. Boone Pickens has shown remarkable leadership in this area. A self-described lifelong oil man, Pickens plans to invest billions of dollars in wind power transmission lines and infrastructure to help free America from our reliance on foreign dictators for energy. From the Texas panhandle to North Dakota, Pickens's plan for wind energy would cost $1.2 trillion to construct. That's a huge investment, but the economic and energy rewards would be even greater. It would provide Americans with cheap, clean, renewable energy on a vast scale. If we are serious about lowering electricity prices, we have to get serious about developing wind energy like never before.

SOLAR POWER

Recent technological advances have made solar energy a major potential resource for America. American and even foreign businesses are starting to take solar power seriously, with firms buying up land for solar projects in the southwest at breakneck speed. From Goldman Sachs and Chevron to Israeli and German solar companies, businesses are already betting their own money that solar power can work.

If all of the 1 million acres currently claimed for solar power were developed, every year it would generate double the amount of electricity needed to power California.

With the right incentives and policies we could see an explosion of solar technology that would fundamentally transform our energy policy forever. The power is there; all it needs is a little help.

BIOFUELS

Biofuels offer us the chance to use our unrivaled agricultural skills to power our economy. For example, we can grow corn, sugar, and other vegetation to produce ethanol to run our cars. In 2007, the United States produced over 6 billion gallons of ethanol, with production expected to rise in the future.[15] Gas stations across the country have begun offering ethanol-gasoline blends such as E85 (85 percent ethanol and 15 percent gasoline), giving us a small but important push toward energy independence. Overall, we have the ability to replace a meaningful percentage of our gasoline consumption with ethanol if we aggressively develop the millions of tons of biomass in the United States.

Additionally, we should explore methanol, another potential alternative to gasoline, and one that's even cheaper per mile and easier to produce on a massive scale than ethanol is.

And the technology to produce biofuels continues to improve. We've learned to make alcohol fuels from sugarcane and cellulosic biomass, both of which produce twice as much ethanol per acre than corn while requiring less irrigation and fertilization.[16] Although we still face some challenges in commercializing cellulosic biomass, it holds great potential.

As we develop new types of fuel, we can expect a rising demand for flexible fuel vehicles (FFVs), which allow drivers to choose what fuel they want to use. FFVs are a great innovation for American drivers because they spark price competition among fuels at the pump.

Led by auto makers General Motors, Chrysler, Nissan, and Ford, ethanol-capable FFVs are now entering the market, with over 1,500 E85 refueling stations already available for FFVs in the United States.[17]

Fuel flexibility offers a tremendous opportunity to lower prices quickly and decrease our need for foreign oil. But we aren't doing nearly enough to take advantage of it. We need to rapidly move toward making fuel flexibility a standard feature in cars, like seatbelts or airbags. This isn't as difficult as it may seem—the ratio of flex-fuel vehicles in Brazil increased from zero to 70 percent of new cars in just three years, and today stands at 90 percent of new cars. As oil prices increase, consumers in Brazil can protect themselves by using alternative fuels. Americans should have the same option.

If we mandate that most new vehicles be flex-fuel, and accompany such a mandate with incentives for creating technology with greater fuel diversity and a refundable tax credit for retooling the auto industry, we could use our abundant domestic resources to end America's dependence on foreign oil, fundamentally changing the balance of power between America and oil exporting cartels.

HYDROGEN

Hydrogen is yet another resource that could potentially transform our energy and environmental future. An American economy that runs on hydrogen would have all the energy it needed with virtually no harmful emissions.

The incredible technology behind this is fuel cells. These use hydrogen to produce huge amounts of electricity—and the only emission is water. Of course, first we have to produce the hydrogen, and that requires energy.

The potential for hydrogen is enormous. Hydrogen fuel cells are two to three times more fuel efficient than the engines we have in our cars today—and the fuel they use is the most abundant element in the universe. Enough hydrogen to fuel a quarter of the world's cars is already produced globally each year, and 70 percent of Americans already live in areas where a hydrogen refueling station could be built within two miles of their home.

Companies are surging ahead with plans for hydrogen cars. BMW now has a dual-fuel hydrogen vehicle, while General Motors, which is also promising a new plug-in hybrid by 2010, aims to have a hydrogen-powered car ready by that same year and in production by 2015. These cars will be more efficient, have one-tenth as many moving parts as current automobiles, and could even be designed to connect to and power more than ten homes during a power outage. All with no emissions.

There are currently forty-five hydrogen refueling stations throughout the United States, with most concentrated in California (25) and Michigan (7).[18] Even more promising, Shell Hydrogen and General Motors just opened the first station with integrated hydrogen and gasoline refueling. Just as companies are charging ahead with hydrogen cars, the government and private businesses are starting to put in place the infrastructure needed for an eventual transition to a hydrogen economy. We're not yet doing enough to push forward hydrogen technology, but we're off to a good start.

PLUG-IN HYBRIDS AND ELECTRIC VEHICLES

We're on the verge of a technological breakthrough with plug-in hybrids that could significantly reduce our dependence on foreign oil. While standard hybrids run on both gasoline and electricity, a plug-in hybrid can travel much further purely on electricity. Because half of Americans don't drive their cars more than thirty-five miles per day, a plug-in hybrid that could run on electricity for thirty-five miles would free millions of Americans from the cost of gasoline nearly every day.

It's also much cheaper to drive a mile on electricity than on gas. Usually, an American driving a plug-in hybrid could expect each mile of electricity to cost one to three pennies compared to twenty cents with gasoline. And because many Americans have garages with electric sockets, plug-in hybrids don't require any real changes in our infrastructure. That's an important consideration that often gets left out of many energy discussions; the more an energy source can use the existing proven infrastructure, the cheaper and faster it can be deployed.

General Motors intends to have a fully electric vehicle that uses no gasoline, called the Chevy Volt, ready for production by 2010. Other carmakers such as Toyota are now competing to create the highest quality plug-in hybrid at the lowest price.

SOLVING THE ENERGY CRISIS
THROUGH NEW SCIENCE

As we've seen, America is truly blessed with vast energy resources. But we haven't yet mentioned the country's greatest energy resource of all: the American people.

We are a highly-educated country filled with scientists, engineers, technicians, and entrepreneurs. Although politicians need to approve the right policies, it's really these people who we're depending on to develop the technological breakthroughs that will lead us out of the energy crisis.

The imminent, enormous advances in science and technology provide a major reason for all of us to be optimistic about our ability to meet the triple challenge of energy, the economy, and the environment in a way that will strengthen our national security.

In the next twenty-five years we will have four to seven times as much new science as we developed in the last twenty-five years. That means we will have more scientific progress than we had in the last hundred years.

The American people instinctively understand this—an American Solutions poll found that 89 percent of Americans believe we will soon have an enormous increase in scientific knowledge.

This potential for bold new breakthroughs is vital to any plan for a better future.

People in America and around the world can have more energy and a better environment at the same time. In fact, a truly rising standard of living for everyone must include exactly those two components. Science and technology is the key to making this a reality.

New science can lead to technological breakthroughs that make the next generation of cars, trucks, airplanes, and other vehicles dramatically lighter and stronger at the same time. The Boeing 787 Dreamliner with its composite construction is an example of this kind of breakthrough. This technology could lead to huge savings in mileage if applied to cars and trucks, while incorporating it in new buildings could lead to radically lower carbon emissions and much lower construction costs.

New science can lead to a dramatic series of breakthroughs in energy sources including plentiful, inexpensive solar cells providing pollution-free distributed energy; new batteries that become 'swap-out' systems that enable you to drive into a service station and swap your depleted battery for a new one in about the time it takes to fill a gas tank; and a host of other improvements.

New science can find better methods of dealing with nuclear waste, new approaches to clean coal, a hydrogen car engine with no pollution, and biological systems of producing gasoline direct from waste material without refining.

The history of the last 200 years has been that one generation's science fiction is the next generation's practical reality.

Before you reject this optimistic vision of a continuously inventing and improving America, try this: pull out your cell phone and look at the camera built into it; look at your ATM card that lets you get money anywhere in the world; turn on your high definition television and click through the several hundred cable channels; or walk to the kitchen and open the microwave oven in which you can heat up a frozen dinner in a few minutes. Now imagine trying to explain any of this to someone 200 years ago, in 1808, when there was no electric light, refrigerators, or telephones.

Welcome to the land of opportunity and invention.

Any strategic plan for energy should have a very powerful component for scientific and technological development.

This doesn't mean pouring more money into Department of Energy bureaucracies with lots of paperwork and little progress.

What it does mean is dramatically expanding H1b visas so good scientists and engineers from around the world can come to America to help make all of us wealthier.

It means creating a permanent research and development tax credit that encourages companies to invest in new breakthroughs.

It means tripling the National Science Foundation budget so grants can be made to laboratory scientists working on real breakthroughs.

It means creating a series of tax-free prizes to incentivize people to invent a better future.

It means creating 100 percent expensing for new technology, new tools, and new laboratories so businesses can write off the investment in one year.

As the world's leader in science and technology, the United States stands to usher in dramatic advances to vastly improve our standard of living. However, we risk falling behind if we don't reform our education system so that every child gets a deeper understanding of math and science. We have to move from "no child left behind" to "every American gets ahead."

Every American should see the film "Two Million Minutes." It's a vivid introduction to the degree to which Chinese and Indian students are being dramatically better educated in math and science than our own children. Visit www.2mminutes.com and you will see what science and math education in America has to become if we are to remain the most productive and creative society in the world.

We have to develop strategies that invest in scientific research instead of trial lawyers, put money in laboratories instead of red tape, and emphasize the exciting possibility of the future rather than simply trying to control the problems of the present.

We CAN do it if we have the WILL to do it.

WE DID IT THEN, AND WE CAN DO IT NOW: A LESSON FROM HISTORY

America has the most coal, oil shale, and wind power potential, the best nuclear technology, and the most advanced car and solar technologies in the world, along with well over 100 billion barrels of oil just waiting to be drilled. Inarguably, we have the power to solve our energy crisis—and solve it soon.

But our critics in the "No-We-Can't" club argue that we can't do anything fast. "We can't affect the price of gasoline for ten years or more" is a typical complaint. Whatever solutions we propose they reject, claiming they're too hard, take too long, or simply can't be done.

Americans who want a fast, decisive solution to our energy problems should recall what we accomplished in World War II.

The time between the Japanese attack at Pearl Harbor on December 7, 1941, and victory over Japan in August 1945 was a mere three years and eight months.

Think about the speed and scale of our actions during that time. In just forty-four months the United States helped defeat Nazi Germany, Fascist Italy, and Imperial Japan.

Our participation in World War II was four months shorter than one presidential term.

It was less than two terms in the House of Representatives.

It was less than two-thirds of one term in the Senate.

Bill Forstchen, Steve Hanser, and I have written two novels about that period, *Pearl Harbor* and *Days of Infamy*. As we studied World War II, we became amazed by how big, fast, comprehensive, and decisive the American effort was.

In those forty-four months America built:

- 102 aircraft carriers
- 5,626 merchant ships
- 273,882 aircraft, including simultaneously producing thousands of the three most powerful heavy bombers:
  - ➤ 12,761 B-17s
  - ➤ 18,481 B-24s
  - ➤ 3,895 B-29s

Our ability to build three different heavy bombers at the same time is key to understanding the right strategy for American energy today. Just as we developed parallel tracks to an atomic bomb, we built parallel bomber systems. We simply did everything we had to do to win decisively.

The various weapons systems required enormous investments in an entire industrial infrastructure that would make America the most powerful industrial country in the world for the following sixty years, right up to today.

It was this systematic approach to solving the problem by doing whatever it took, no matter how large the scale, that made our actions in World War II so incredible. Consider:

- America built a vast industrial infrastructure from scratch. Hundreds of factories sprang up, many deliberately situated in the Midwest so they would be out of range of feared transcontinental bombers.
- When enemy ships sank our tankers at a phenomenal rate early in the war, a pipeline was hurriedly laid from Texas to New York to help transport fuel to the frontlines.
- Shipyards that had been rust yards in the 1930s turned out thousands of transports and fighting ships. Tens of thousands of landing craft, ranging from the famed Higgins boat to huge tank landing ships designed to haul thousands of tons straight onto a beach, came out in a flood of production. At one shipyard, Liberty ships were sliding out of the assembly line at a rate of one per day.
- More than a quarter million military aircraft were manufactured, from small 65-horsepower trainers and recon birds up to huge B-29 Superfortresses. Over

30,000 of them were heavy bombers; more than a hundred thousand were fighters. And just as important, hundreds of thousands of men were given the technical training to fly them, fly them well, and fly them to victory.

- Entire cities that could hold tens of thousands of people were fabricated in deserts, tropical atolls, and in the arctic wilderness to house troops on distant fronts and provide support for the frontlines. Floating cities of thousands of specialized transports, supply ships, repair ships, hospital ships, and ammunition ships kept battle task forces of hundreds of warships afloat and in the fight. It was a logistical feat unrivaled in history.

- Cities to house hundreds of thousands were built from scratch in Tennessee, New Mexico, and Washington State for those working on the most secret of all programs, the Manhattan Project. Starting with nothing more than a few theoretical papers and a couple dozen scientists and engineers, within four years Americans cracked the atom and created a weapon that, though horrifying, brought an end to the war and held the promise of providing near limitless energy.

- More than 15 million Americans went into uniform and were equipped with rations, medical support, and weapons. They were put in ships and airplanes, transported half way around the world to fight, returned back home, and then rewarded with the famed G.I. Bill of Rights, which transformed post-war America.

● The Pentagon did not exist in 1940. Yet, by the summer of 1941 the War Department had over 24,000 people, both military and civilian, working in seventeen different buildings. The original plan was to build temporary buildings to house the growing workforce, but Brigadier General Brehon Somervell proposed a different approach. On July 17, 1941, he gave two of his subordinates four days to submit plans for an air conditioned office building that could hold 40,000 workers. They did it. The following day, the Secretary of War approved the plan and informed President Roosevelt while Brigadier General Somervell submitted the plan to Congress. Funding was provided through a supplemental defense appropriations bill that summer. Construction began on September 11, 1941, and the basic shell and roof were complete in one year. In sixteen months the entire project was finished—a task that would have normally taken four years.

The country operated this fast and this effectively because Americans were determined to win. As President Roosevelt pronounced the day after the attack on Pearl Harbor, "With confidence in our armed forces, with the unbounding determination of our people, we will gain the inevitable triumph, so help us God."

The challenge today of loosening the chains of our dependence on unsavory foreign sources of energy pales in comparison to the challenge Americans faced in 1940—and overcame.

To solve today's energy crisis, we can and should expand all our existing systems of energy, while simultaneously developing new energy sources and new systems of conservation.

All that is needed is leadership and a determined national will to see the job done.

FOUR

WE CAN DO IT

A ROADMAP FOR AFFORDABLE, ABUNDANT AMERICAN ENERGY

Americans want to recapture the "can do, get it done, cut through the red tape" attitude that our parents and grandparents displayed in World War II. This could help us achieve a set of key goals:

- the development of American energy resources to bring down prices
- the use of American technology to increase energy conservation, create alternative fuels, and better protect the environment
- the development of new methods for the production and conservation of oil and natural gas to liberate America from its dependence on foreign dictatorships

Simply put, Americans want to do it all, do it now, and do it for America.

Americans reject tiresome arguments about false tradeoffs between conservation and the development of oil and natural gas. We want it all done at the same time and with the same intensity of speed and effort.

Americans want action now because we are deeply worried by all the indicators of economic breakdown and financial stress we see around us.

Americans are first and foremost worried about the impact of high energy prices on our own lives and family budgets. But we are also worried about the increasingly stressed airline industry and the very real threat of it collapsing under the pressure of high aviation fuel prices.

We are worried that the ripple effect of high prices for trucking, travel, and petroleum- and natural gas-based manufacturing may lead to a big jump in inflation.

Americans have watched the stock market slide into bear market levels as the combination of the subprime mess, the shaky financial system, and the high price of oil and natural gas all pound on the values of our savings, pension plans, and retirement hopes.

The great lesson of World War II is to do it all and do it fast.

We need more development of American oil, oil shale, and gas reserves.

We need a dramatically greater effort to develop our coal and natural gas reserves and to explore the possibility of using them as new gasoline and diesel substitutes.

We need to pursue clean coal and nuclear power as primary sources of electrical power that lower costs and protect the environment.

We need to diversify American sources of electricity generation so that we don't increase dependence on foreign natural gas producers that could develop an OPEC-like natural gas cartel.

We need to expand the world of alternatives like wind, solar, hydrogen, biofuels, hybrids, and other cost-effective, environmentally sound technologies.

We need flex-fuel vehicles so that "we the consumer" can decide which fuel we want to use and not be trapped into any one fuel source by either politicians or bureaucrats.

And we need to enact legislation to end the culture of litigation that is contributing to the problem. For example, an environmental extremist group is suing to block BP from expanding its oil refinery capacity in Whiting, Indiana, an expansion that would bring an additional 620 million gallons of gas to U.S. consumers each year. This is happening even though there are no sensitive environmental issues involved. Other refinery expansions are delayed for similar reasons.

This is the broad range of goals we should adopt to put us on the path to energy independence.

What we also need is a Manhattan Project for energy breakthroughs—a program to foster bold scientific innovations and transform them into engineering achievements in record time.

As it turns out, there is a proposal in Congress to create just such a project: Congressman Randy Forbes's bill for a "New Manhattan Project for Energy Independence" (HR 6260). This calls for the creation of a scientific commission that would develop a plan to have us 50 percent energy independent in ten years and 100 percent independent in twenty.

Crucially, the bill depends on the private sector, innovative entrepreneurs, and our brightest engineers and academics to devise solutions. The government plays a critical role by helping them with grants and sparking competition by offering huge cash prizes for the key breakthroughs. In the end, however, a new Manhattan Project for energy can only work if it depends on the unparalleled innovation and resourcefulness of the American people.

A Manhattan Project for energy requires that the government set a clear vision with concrete goals and provide the incentives and grants to achieve them. If we challenge the American people to devote their best and brightest citizens to solving this crisis, it can be done faster than we ever imagined possible. But we need leadership and a bold vision for energy independence from our government for such a project to succeed.

A ROADMAP FOR SOLVING OUR ENERGY CRISIS

So how do we get started on solving our energy crisis? Once we acknowledge that we can, in fact, overcome the energy crisis, we see that the specific solutions are all within our grasp. What follows is a point-by-point plan for lowering energy costs and creating cleaner, more abundant energy.

SOLUTIONS FOR MORE OIL AND
NATURAL GAS DEVELOPMENT

1. **Change federal law to allow offshore drilling for oil and natural gas**. This is a necessary first step that will help lower oil and natural gas prices in the short and long term.

2. **Change federal law to allow drilling for oil and natural gas in the Alaskan National Wildlife Refuge (ANWR).** This is a necessary first step that will allow for the development of the most easily accessible known oil reserves in the United States.

3. **Change federal law to allow for development of oil shale in Utah, Wyoming and Colorado.** This is a necessary first step that will signal American willingness to develop one of our most plentiful energy resources. Right now, Congress prohibits the Department of the Interior (DOI) from using any funding to finish writing regulations for issuing leases to companies for oil shale exploration. The ban also stops the DOI from finalizing an environmental impact statement required before any oil shale development can begin. Lifting this moratorium will allow the DOI to finalize the regulations and complete the environmental study so we can expand oil shale development.

4. **Change federal law to incentivize those states that want to permit energy exploration to do so with appropriate safeguards.**

5.   **Change federal law to give all states with offshore oil and gas the same share of federal royalties as most states get for land-based resources (48 percent).** Today most states get zero royalties from offshore oil and gas development, while states like Wyoming earn 48 percent of federal royalties for its land-based oil and gas. If Richmond, Tallahassee, and Sacramento suddenly had the potential to find billions of dollars a year in new revenues for their state budgets, their willingness to embrace new oil and gas development with appropriate environmental safeguards would probably increase dramatically.

A share of the state and federal revenues from new offshore development could be set aside to finance biodiversity investments and national park infrastructure projects. Additional revenues could fund infrastructure projects like new roads, bridges, inland waterways, environment-enhancing water projects, public transit, and a new, more efficient, satellite-based air traffic control system. The amount of new revenue from tapping our own resources would be large enough to do these things while helping to offset the costs of research and development of alternative energy sources.

6.   **Create public/private partnerships in coastal states to fast track the ability of oil and natural gas companies to develop offshore oil and gas resources.** If Congress were to lift the ban on offshore oil and gas development (or at least grant coastal states the op-

tion to develop the resources, providing they share the revenues with the federal government), states would move swiftly to set up partnerships that will maximize the best use of oil and gas revenues.

Efforts in Virginia provide a good example. In 2004, two Virginia legislators, Delegate Chris Saxman and Senator Frank Wagner, learned that Virginia manufacturers were warning of the rising costs of energy because of tightening energy supplies. Upon discovering that oil and gas resources exist off Virginia's shores, and that the state could experience rapid economic development from the business of energy exploration and development, Saxman and Wagner immediately designed legislation that would have Virginia petition the federal government for permits to drill offshore. Additionally, the legislation specified that a significant portion of oil and gas royalties, state fees, and licenses collected by the state would go to improve Virginia's transportation infrastructure, clean up the Chesapeake Bay, and invest in technologies related to new energy production.

The economic potential for Virginia is significant. The oil and natural gas revenue estimated to accrue to Virginia is $13.53 billion dollars over thirty years, or $451 million annually. This is a conservative estimate that could increase with technological advances.

But these are not all the economic benefits that Virginia would reap. In just the Hampton Roads area near Norfolk, it is estimated, based on experience with the oil and gas industry in Nova Scotia and Louisiana, that oil and natural gas development would result in around $8 billion in capital investment and 2,600 new, high-paying jobs. These new jobs would have an estimated payroll close to $650 million annually. Virginia would thus see $271 million more flow into the state treasury in the form of state and local taxes as a result of this increased economic activity.

This new tax revenue could then be used to fund transportation projects in the Hampton Roads area and throughout the state.

Imagine funding new roads, cleaning up the environment, and making investments in basic research and development science to promote new energy sources—all without raising taxes. How many coastal states besides Virginia would like to realize those benefits? Coastal states could lower energy costs for their residents as well as the energy costs of fellow citizens across the country, while relieving congestion and cleaning up the environment.

All told, Virginia would stand to gain $722 million more in annual revenue if drilling were permitted offshore.

Unfortunately, anti-energy elites in the Virginia Senate blocked the measure by a single vote.

7. **Consider ways to distribute the benefits of drilling to every citizen.** One major reason Alaskan residents support drilling is that the benefits of it reach their

own pockets. Alaskans receive a check every year from a dividend fund established in 1976 to distribute state revenues from drilling leases (as long as there is interest on the principal). As of 2007, the state had $37.8 billion in the fund. This allows residents to reap the financial benefits of drilling even beyond lower gas prices.

Other states should consider adopting similar programs to benefit their own residents. Just imagine a flood of checks and tax cuts across the nation as states with offshore, onshore, and oil shale drilling share their new wealth with their residents. This would be a remarkable way to boost economic growth.

8. **Allow companies engaged in oil and gas exploration and development to write off their investments in one year by expensing all of it against their tax liabilities.** This will lead to an explosion of new exploration and development.

9. **If Congress lifts the ban on drilling offshore and in ANWR, then it should simultaneously release up to one-tenth of the Strategic Petroleum Reserve (SPR).** This should be accompanied by a promise to dedicate the federal revenues from the sales to replenishing the reserves with future American oil production. This will likely have an immediate effect on oil prices, as was the case in 1991. In that year, President George H. W. Bush announced his intention to open the reserve and oil prices immediately dropped almost $11 per barrel.

10. **Restore the oil shale provisions of the Energy Policy Act of 2005.** This would ensure that anything that was affected by the Congressional moratorium continues as though the moratorium were never approved.

11. **Until drilling in ANWR is permitted, allow participating oil companies to do seismic surveys to find out how much oil is in the 10-02 area of ANWR's Coastal Plain.** Oil companies should be allowed to discover how much oil is in this area, which is the section thought to contain the most oil. This could be done in one winter season with minimal impact on the environment, and it would be funded by the oil companies, which would make the information public. If the American people discovered how much oil there really was in this area of ANWR, Congress would face renewed pressure to lift the moratorium, while oil companies would get an even bigger incentive to begin drilling as soon as possible.

SOLUTIONS FOR REFINERIES

12. **Give companies an incentive to build refineries and increase capacity by shortening the depreciation schedule**. Right now, it's so expensive and time-consuming to build a refinery that most companies don't even try. When companies build refineries or expand old ones, they are allowed to write off the cost of the equipment over a ten-year period, meaning a company has to wait ten years to recover the cost of that equipment. This is called depreciation.

We should immediately change the tax code so that a company that builds or expands a refinery can receive the benefits of depreciation within five years. This will give companies a big incentive to start building.

13. **Allow companies to write off 100 percent of their expenses in the first year if their new refineries or additions significantly expand America's total refining capacity.** The 2005 Energy Act had a provision that let companies write off 50 percent of expenses in the first year if the refineries increased capacity, but it took the IRS three years before it came up with the rules to enact this law. For three years companies were scared to build refineries because they didn't know if they were ever going to get the benefit of this provision. We should make this provision retroactive so that companies that began building during the last three years can receive the benefits and not be punished by the IRS's incompetence. Then, we should further enlarge the incentive to build refineries and expand existing capacity by increasing the amount companies can write off in their first year to cover the entire cost of the equipment.

14. **Enact real litigation reform for companies building refineries or expanding capacity.** As explained later in this chapter, a loser-pays rule in litigation would help cut down on frivolous lawsuits dramatically. In the case of Arizona Clean Fuels, this kind of reform could have prevented a lawsuit, later dismissed as

frivolous, that cost the company some $500,000 in legal expenses, forcing it to change locations to escape the debilitating financial and time delays. Lawsuits are a huge problem for refinery projects, and we can't expect more to be built as long as lawsuits can hold up projects for years at a time and frustrate efforts to finance new refineries.

15. **Make the permitting process for building a refinery or expanding capacity easier and faster.** The current permitting process involves submitting applications for various permits to multiple agencies and takes years to complete. Senator Pete Domenici (R-NM) has introduced legislation that would allow the EPA to accept permit applications that put all the permits needed to build and operate refineries together into one package. The proposal also forces regulators to act on applications for new refineries within a year, with a 120-day limit for deciding on applications to expand old ones.

SOLUTIONS FOR MORE, CLEANER COAL

16. **Immediately renegotiate the FutureGen clean coal project for Illinois to get it built as rapidly as possible.** It is utterly irrational for the Department of Energy to postpone the most advanced clean coal project in America.

17. **Launch three more competitive clean coal plants on a competitive bid, incentivized, fast-track basis**

with specific metrics of achievements to be rewarded. Clean coal would be such an important breakthrough for the environment, and coal is such an enormous American resource, that it is worth launching four parallel pilot projects immediately. This was precisely the Manhattan Project approach in World War II.

18. **Save time by allowing construction of experimental clean coal plants on brownfields in already industrialized areas without complex environmental regulations.** Ohio Congressman Mike Turner shows the right approach in his proposed legislation to protect green areas by encouraging redevelopment of existing industrial areas.

19. **Congress should approve a series of tax-free prizes to accelerate innovation in developing new technologies for using coal.** The result will be a better environment, more energy independence, and more energy at lower cost. Eliminate half the Department of Energy bureaucracy and use the savings to fund the prizes. America will get a much bigger, faster return on its investment.

20. **Develop a tax credit for refitting existing coal plants.** A lot of existing coal plants are going to be around for a long time. The most efficient way to make them more environmentally acceptable is to create a tax credit for retrofitting them with new methods and new technologies.

SOLUTIONS FOR MORE NUCLEAR POWER

21. **Pass a streamlined regulatory regime and a favorable tax regime for building a new generation of safe nuclear reactors**. Nuclear power can help create a dramatically better future for the environment and for domestic energy production. Nuclear power plants are especially valuable because they can produce the same amount of energy twenty-four hours a day and therefore can produce hydrogen for a hydrogen-powered automobile system at night when the electricity grid doesn't need the power. Thus, a significant increase in nuclear technology is also a helpful step toward a hydrogen economy.

22. **Accelerate research and development in Generation IV nuclear power plants**. As described in Chapter 3, we must do all we can to make sure this project is completed as soon as possible by offering the right prizes and incentives for development.

23. **Provide a prize for safe disposal or reuse of nuclear waste products**. Congressman Burgess has proposed awarding a prize to any individual or company that can develop an alternative means for storing high level nuclear waste. Now a part of the American Energy Act (H.R. 6566), the legislation would authorize the Secretary of Energy to annually award two, $10 million prizes tax-free through 2020. Instead of obligating the government to fund these awards, the legislation would authorize the Department of Energy

to raise funds for the award through the support of private entities. Although Yucca Mountain has a proposed storage facility for nuclear waste, industry analysts predict that by 2015 the United States will have to accommodate the storage of 70,000 tons of high-level nuclear byproduct. If the U.S. builds more power plants, this award will play a critical role in identifying an alternative to Yucca that would help make nuclear energy storage more efficient, clean, and practical.

SOLUTIONS FOR MORE ALTERNATIVE POWER

24. **Make the solar power and wind power tax credits permanent to create a large-scale industry dedicated to domestically produced renewable electricity.** We have enormous opportunities in solar, wind, and other renewable electricity sources that can be developed with a stable tax policy.

25. **Develop long-distance transmission lines to move wind power from the Great Plains wind belt to Chicago and other urban centers.** We could generate an enormous amount of electricity generation from wind, but it's locked up geographically because the neighboring states have no incentive to be helpful. Potentially, Chicago could use the power generated in the Dakotas, while West Texas could generate the electricity East Texas needs. The federal government may have to help make the connections possible.

SOLUTIONS IN TRANSPORTATION

26. **Allow auto companies to use refundable tax credits for the cost of flex-fuels cars, hybrids, plug-in hybrids, and the development of hydrogen cars, including necessary retooling for manufacturing.** U.S. auto companies get billions in tax credits. However, the firms aren't making any profits, and thus they can't turn the tax credits into useful money. The federal government could solve this problem by making the tax credits refundable if they're spent on helping to solve the energy problem. This would be a win-win strategy of much greater importance than the ongoing fight over CAFE rules, which set fuel efficiency standards for new cars without any incentives to achieve them.

27. **Create an Open Fuel Standard for 95 percent of the new cars sold in the United States.** An Open Fuel Standard would ensure that most new cars sold in America are flex-fuel vehicles (FFVs) that can use a variety of fuel types. It costs less than $100 extra to build a car as an FFV as compared to gasoline-only, and this will provide Americans fuel choice and price competition at the pump. Furthermore, the federal government needs to provide tax credits to help auto companies cope with the transition costs to flex fuel, and Congress needs to streamline the regulations and certification requirements for the transition.

28. **Approve tax incentives for new fuel distribution stations.** There should be a substantial tax break for

investing in both ethanol and hydrogen supply stations as well as hydrogen pipelines so the fuel can
be delivered at a reasonable cost when flex-fuel cars
come on the market.

29. **Approve tax incentives for composite manufacturing**. There ought to be a tax credit for car companies
to retool in favor of composite materials manufacturing, which will radically lower the weight of cars
and improve gas mileage. UPS has ordered experimental composite delivery vans that reduce weight
by 2,000 pounds and increase mileage by 30 percent.
Some have estimated that composite materials
combined with a hybrid E-85 engine could produce
a vehicle that could run for 500 to 1,000 miles on one
gallon of petroleum.

30. **Approve tax incentives for turning in old, polluting
cars**. This would help the poor, the environment,
and the ailing American auto industry.

31. **Approve a billion-dollar tax-free prize for the first
hydrogen car that can be mass-produced for a reasonable price**. A successful America focuses on investing in a better future and knows that customers
will rapidly switch to new, superior products. The
same is true for creating a new energy strategy. We
need very large prizes for fundamental breakthroughs. Hydrogen has to be the ultimate basis for
a truly bold energy prize because it has no environmental impact and is universally available as a natural resource. Therefore, a mass-produced hydrogen

car would have huge appeal to China and India if it were reasonably priced. American technologies for hydrogen vehicles might be one of the biggest economic winners of the next generation.

32. **Dramatically increase funding to develop hydrogen fuel cells.** A National Research Council report found that if the government is willing to invest an average of $11 billion per year on hydrogen technology and infrastructure between now and 2050, 100 percent of all cars and light trucks in the U.S. could be hydrogen-powered with zero emissions by 2050. This might seem like a lot of money at first, but it's nothing compared to the incredible advantages of a hydrogen economy, including our retention of the $700 billion per year we're paying to foreign countries for oil. By increasing funding we could have 25 million hydrogen-powered cars on the road by 2030 and be well on our way to a revolution in our energy and environmental policy that will give Americans more energy at lower costs.

SOLUTIONS TO REMOVE BUREAUCRATIC ROADBLOCKS

33. **Streamline agency reviews of drilling projects.** The delay and confusion caused by bureaucracies often stems from a lack of coordination among the huge number of government agencies.

    For onshore drilling projects, there are at least eight agencies spread across four departments involved in the approval process. The problem is that every agency only focuses on doing its own job without considering the big picture. For example, the Environmental Protection Agency only cares about making sure the Clean Air Act or the Clean Water Act is being enforced. As long as it meets that responsibility, it's simply not concerned that it may be causing massive delays throughout the rest of the system because other agencies are waiting for it to finish its job before they can do theirs.

We need a fundamental restructuring of the bureaucracy at the local branch level so that all the agencies involved in approving drill leases and permits work in one office together and report to one boss who oversees and coordinates all their efforts.

This reform has already been tested with incredible success. The 2005 Energy Act created a pilot program to consolidate a few local branches of these agencies in various locations. Two years later, the results speak for themselves. In 2006, the offices that participated in the program processed 73 percent of the applications for drilling permits, compared to just 27 percent handled by the offices that retained the old bureaucratic structure.

As efficiency rose, so did environmental oversight—in 2007, the pilot offices completed 100 percent of their planned inspections for the year. While it isn't unusual for offices to conduct all their planned inspections, what makes the pilot office numbers so impressive is that their inspections were much more in-depth and wide-ranging than the non-pilot inspections. They met their inspection goals while improving the quality of the inspections.

This reform leads to dramatically fewer delays, less cost to energy companies, better relationships between agencies, and improved environmental protection. It is a commonsense solution that we should implement immediately for both onshore and offshore drilling.

34. **Dramatically increase the funding and staff levels of these offices.** Often suffering from severe shortages of personnel and money, these government offices must be given the resources needed to do their jobs.

35. **Save one year in duplicative paperwork in processing drilling applications.** When an oil company goes through the process of trying to drill offshore, the Minerals Management Service (MMS), which oversees offshore drilling regulations, has to create a five-year plan that includes a host of different steps and environmental analyses and takes two to three years to finish.

There are three very long steps in this process during which the MMS publishes its proposal for the methods and location of the drilling. The first step is called the "draft proposed program," which is followed by the "proposed program," and eventually leads to the publication of the "final proposed program."

Here's what this really means: the MMS first says what it plans to do, then what it really plans to do, and finally, what it really, really plans to do.

This inefficient process has led the Outer Continental Shelf policy committee to suggest eliminating the "draft proposed program" step. It's possible that this simple reform will save energy companies and federal agencies *one year* in paperwork and planning time. We should immediately enact this recommendation.

36. **Make agency behavior transparent and accountable**. If every agency had to publish information every week on how many applications it was processing, how long they had been in process, and other key indicators, there would be dramatic pressure not to be the most inefficient agency. Congress would also know how to evaluate which agencies required more oversight or resources.

There are several other important bureaucratic reforms that should be enacted and even more radical steps to consider, but these examples highlight how small, commonsense solutions can lead to dramatically fewer delays and costs that will lead to more energy and lower prices. Untangling the web of bureaucracy that chokes off oil development is difficult, but we can't hope to solve the energy crisis if we don't commit to real change to a bureaucratic system that is clearly broken.

SOLUTIONS TO REDUCE LITIGATION

37. **Empower government agencies to fight off frivolous lawsuits.** The likelihood that any drilling permit

given to a company will be challenged in court greatly exacerbates our nation's energy crisis. An environment where hostile interest groups frequently challenge drilling permits for ridiculous reasons is one in which there is less drilling and less energy for the American people.

Our government is a highly complex organization that is impossible for Congress to fully manage. So when Congress passes a law setting certain goals or requiring different procedures to be used by an agency, it usually leaves it up to that agency to decide how best to implement the law. For complicated historical reasons, this is not the case with the agencies that regulate drilling.

In 1969, Congress passed the National Environmental Policy Act (NEPA) requiring that agencies follow certain procedures when deciding the methods and locations for oil drilling. The bill is purposefully vague and doesn't define a lot of important phrases and words, which is not unusual for legislation.

Typically, Congress writes somewhere in a new law that the agencies responsible for implementing it can interpret the law's language based on their own expertise and experience. Unfortunately, NEPA didn't do that. As a result, anti-drilling environmental extremist, when challenging whether a government agency followed NEPA regulations, often argue that the agency's actions are inconsistent with the law's language. Unfortunately, activist courts often side with the extremists and rule that the agencies don't have the authority to define the law's language. Instead, the courts decide that only they can define these words.

The result is a system of regulations that have been largely written by the courts—which have no experience or expertise in energy at all—in ways that hinder the activities of both energy-related agencies and energy companies.

This has led agencies to try to create "appeal-proof" environmental assessments in which they far exceed the necessary environmental protections in order to make it harder for environmental extremists to win lawsuits. However, even these costly and time-consuming "appeal-proof" assessments frequently lose in court. In 2006, out of 108 lawsuits filed under NEPA against government agencies, courts ordered injunctions or ordered the case to be remanded in two-thirds of cases. All this means less drilling, more delays, and more ridiculous regulations and lawsuits.

The way to fix this crucial problem and stop a lot of frivolous lawsuits is to pass a law that gives the agencies in charge of implementing NEPA regulations the authority to define important words and phrases that Congress left vague. This would be no different than what Congress does for almost every other piece of legislation, and it would greatly limit the courts' power to overrule the decisions these agencies make based on their own considerable expertise.

38. **Implement a loser-pays law for lawsuits challenging drilling permits.** Even if we make it harder for environmental extremists to win lawsuits, they'll probably keep filing one suit after another in hopes of slowing the process down and, ultimately, winning in some liberal activist court.

To stop these baseless lawsuits we need to create a significant incentive not to file them. The best way to do that is to implement a loser-pays law. This means that whichever side loses a lawsuit challenging a drilling permit has to pay all the legal costs for the other side. If an extreme environmentalist group wants to stop all drilling in Alaska by filing frivolous lawsuits challenging drilling permits, and then loses those suits, it should have to pay the legal costs that the government spent defending the permit in court. With a loser-pays law, you would see a dramatic decline in the number of frivolous lawsuits, as there would finally be a real penalty for filing suits that have little chance of success.

This reform would not cause harm to the environment. The vast majority of these lawsuits are frivolous, geared more toward shutting down drilling altogether than ensuring that regulations are followed. In most cases, the environment is being adequately protected by existing regulations, which are rigorously enforced. A loser-pays law would simply encourage activists to stop filing lawsuits unless they have strong evidence of real environmental or regulatory problems. This would actually increase accountability because the courts and the government would take the few lawsuits that were filed much more seriously.

We can protect the environment and cut down on wasteful litigation at the same time. If we want more energy and lower prices, we need real change in our legal system to stop frivolous lawsuits that cause unnecessary delays and cost billions of dollars to energy companies and to taxpayers. It must be a priority in any solution to the energy crisis.

REMEMBER

We can do it all.
We can do it now.
We can do it for America.
This is the American way.

We have stuck to this belief for 400 years, and it has made us the most prosperous and free country in the world.

Let's apply American ingenuity to solving an American problem by developing more American energy now.

FIVE

THE BEST OF BOTH WORLDS

PROTECTING THE ENVIRONMENT WHILE PRODUCING MORE ENERGY

We can produce more American energy and protect the environment at the same time. Contrary to the claims of environmental extremists, these are not opposing interests.

The key is that we pursue:

- conservation policies that make sense.
- more energy efficiency so we can do more with less.
- a smarter, more balanced approach to government regulations.
- better use of our natural resources to protect the environment.
- new scientific breakthroughs, including some dramatic new remediation technologies.

CONSERVATISM *IS* ENVIRONMENTALISM

Before I discuss the pro-American energy, pro-environment approach, I want to say a few words about how I came to believe in it and why I think it's so important for the future of our country.

I first became interested in conservation when I was a kid in Pennsylvania. As a child I originally wanted to be either a zoo director or a paleontologist because I was fascinated by the natural world—and still am. In 1971, I participated in the second Earth Day and became the coordinator of an interdisciplinary environmental studies program at West Georgia College.

In my commitment to the environment, I was echoing the conviction of two well-known Republican leaders. The first is President Theodore Roosevelt, who said that "the nation behaves well if it treats the natural resources as assets, which it must turn over to the next generation increased, and not impaired, in value." The other was then–governor Ronald Reagan who, upon the occasion of the first Earth Day, affirmed the "absolute necessity of waging all-out war against the debauching of the environment."

Conservatives have a well-established historical tradition of caring for the environment because we understand the heavy responsibility that every generation has to pass on a natural world that is just as beautiful and vibrant as the one it inherited. I have believed this truth all my life, and I don't think we have to choose between our environmental responsibilities to the next generation and our duty to provide a strong and robust economy here at home.

Establishing an intellectual and policy framework for a twenty-first-century "Green Conservatism" is a task very near to my heart, and is the subject of a book I co-wrote with Terry Maple, *A Contract with the Earth*.

THE FALSE TRADEOFF BETWEEN PRODUCING ENERGY AND PROTECTING THE ENVIRONMENT

You may have noticed that I used the word "conservation" to describe my environmentalism. This reflects my fundamental disagreement with today's environmental extremists. I believe we should be good stewards of the natural world—we should "conserve" it for our benefit and our children's and grandchildren's benefit, not use it as an excuse for massively expanding regulation, litigation, and bureaucracy.

For the last thirty-eight years, I have watched the anti-energy, pro-regulation, pro-litigation, pro-taxation environmental extremists label themselves as the only Americans who care about the environment.

These extremists would have you believe that to protect clean air and water, biodiversity, and the future of the earth, we have to buy into their catastrophic scenarios and sign on to their command-and-control, anti-energy, big-bureaucracy agenda, which calls for dramatic increases in government power and draconian policies that will devastate our economy.

This is just extremism. The truth is that we can produce more American energy and do it responsibly. Of course, we will not—and cannot—eliminate all risk of harm to the environment as we produce more energy. All energy sources have risks, but the key is to take measures to minimize them. More important, it's vital that we understand and appreciate the extent to which we've already reduced environmental risks thanks to technological innovation. Later in this chapter, we'll see how we've been able to do so with onshore and offshore oil and gas production, nuclear power, oil shale, and increasingly with coal.

The bottom line is that there's a pro-American energy and pro-environment approach that is a better choice for our economy and our environment than the bureaucratic, litigation-focused approach of environmental extremism.

COMMONSENSE ENVIRONMENTALISM VS. ENVIRONMENTAL EXTREMISM

For too long, commonsense citizens have not energetically put forward our own solutions for the environment, while environmental extremists have dominated the debate with ill-conceived regulations, a focus on litigation instead of science, and a preference for taxes over markets and incentives. Mainstream environmentalists have allowed the extremists to hold the high ground on a subject of great concern to all Americans. With your help, I want to change that.

We're obligated to call out outlandish, fear-mongering exaggerations about our environmental future. But for decades mainstream environmentalists have tried to do this without offering an alternative, commonsense vision for conservation.

For example, no responsible scientist anywhere believed a certain former national leader when he suggested that global warming is so bad that we could have a twenty-foot rise in the oceans in the near future. But if all we do is oppose the radical and irresponsible policies of environmental extremists, we end up in a defensive position that allows the extremists to portray us as being anti-environment. We must lead with a sensible approach to the environment that is both pro-energy and pro-environment.

We must make our core argument absolutely clear: you can be totally committed to American principles—individual liberty, a market economy, entrepreneurship, and lower taxes—and still be pro-environment. With the sound use of science and technology and the right incentives to encourage entrepreneurs, American principles will provide a better solution for the health of our planet than will environmental extremism.

So what is involved in a commonsense approach to the environment? Here are the basic values:

- Clean air and clean water.
- A belief in biodiversity as a positive good.
- A position that is pro-science, pro-technology, and pro-innovation, an American combination that has improved lives for four hundred years.
- A belief that we have to favor more American energy production and environmental conservation at the same time, and that this combination is absolutely central to the future of the human race.
- A recognition that economic growth and environmental health are compatible in both the developed and developing worlds.
- An understanding that by shifting tax code incentives and market behavior, we will realize more positive

environmental outcomes faster than we would by
embracing the punishing effects of litigation and regulation.

- A recognition that we have to take seriously the potential risks of climate change and take reasonable
steps today to minimize carbon emissions. This can be
done in a pro-business and pro-growth way that relies
on technology and innovation.

To develop an approach that favors both more American energy
and environmental conservation, we need a comprehensive
strategy to transition gradually from the unimproved fossil fuels
that dramatically improved the quality of life in the past to new
fuels that promise clean, renewable energy for the future. We
need a new generation of clean energy that will help us achieve
the following goals:

- Improving national security by liberating ourselves
from dependence on dangerous dictatorships.
- Boosting our competitiveness in the world economy.
- Creating a cleaner and healthier environment.

Reliable, affordable energy is indispensable to economic growth
around the planet, and economic growth is essential to a healthier environment. Only with a comprehensive approach to both
the environment and the economy can we protect our natural
habitat while ensuring a prosperous America.

DEBUNKING THE CRITICS
OF OFFSHORE DRILLING

When people say that drilling offshore would destroy our oceans and damage our beaches, don't believe it. They are wrong, and our environmental record for offshore oil and gas drilling proves it.

Here are a few numbers for you to consider. A National Research Council report found that 95 percent of the oil that goes into the Gulf of Mexico, where we have the most offshore drilling, is released naturally by the earth from oil seeps; only about 5 percent stems from human activities.[1] And 97 percent of all spills from drilling offshore consist of one barrel of oil or less, according to the Minerals Management Service (MMS). In fact, there hasn't been a major spill from offshore drilling since 1980.

The Royal Society of Canada studied the annual risk of a large oil spill resulting from offshore drilling and found that the chances are about 1 in 10,000, or 0.0001 percent per well.[2] That means there's a 99.9999 percent chance each year that there will be no significant oil spill from any given offshore well. And that estimate didn't even consider all kinds of advances in technology or all the regulations that apply to drilling in the United States. So the real risk is probably much lower.

The risk of a significant spill from an oil tanker in U.S. waters is also low. MMS data show that for every 1 billion barrels of oil that were transported by tankers in U.S. waters from 1985 to 1999, there were just 0.73 spills of 1,000 barrels or more.

And even when a large oil spill does occur, it doesn't necessarily mean we're going to see thousands of dead fish washed up on the beach. A Coast Guard study looked at the likely impact of small, medium, and large spills on an extensive list of organisms that could be affected by the oil in every region offshore. It found that in the Atlantic, Pacific, and Gulf of Mexico, there was never more than a moderate risk to organisms, and the risk was almost always minimal even for large spills.[3] This is important since these are three of the areas where the most offshore drilling would occur if the moratorium were lifted.

Aside from oil spills, extreme environmentalists frequently decry how much mercury is dumped into the oceans because of offshore drilling. Of course, they never mention the fact that drill rigs discharge about 0.7 percent as much mercury into the Gulf of Mexico as the Mississippi River does. And you would never know from listening to these extremists that an MMS study found that the level of mercury in marine organisms around rigs was no higher than the level in organisms further away, or that a thorough experiment out of the Florida Institute of Technology showed that levels of methylmercury, a dangerous form of mercury, around oil rigs were no higher than in other areas. You wouldn't know, in other words, that mercury contamination from offshore drilling isn't a real problem.

Some environmental advocacy groups have objected to offshore oil drilling because of the seismic surveys that companies conduct before they drill. In deciding where to drill, companies have to know where the oil is. From a boat, they shoot low-frequency waves at the ocean floor to determine where the most oil might be. There has been a lot of controversy about whether these seismic waves hurt whales and fish, with extremists claiming that the waves cause whale strandings and destroy fish and whale hearing.

But evidence points to seismic surveys being relatively safe for fish and whales. A background paper prepared for the British Columbia Seafood Alliance states that fish avoid the area where a survey is being conducted and therefore do not have any long-term hearing damage.[4] Another report found that the studied fish population levels were not harmed by seismic waves at all.[5]

There is absolutely no firm evidence that seismic waves permanently harm whale hearing or cause strandings, and research into temporary hearing damage shows that the risk of this happening is minimal in almost all marine mammals.

LGL Environmental Associates concluded that evidence showing that whale hearing is permanently damaged by seismic waves is thin.[6] That same review and a separate one from MMS found that evidence connecting whale strandings to seismic surveys is weak and inconclusive. Usually, environmental extremists concede that evidence for strandings is thin, and instead they try to show that sonar causes strandings. There is a lot more evidence that this is true, and extremists bring it up in hopes that people will confuse sonar with seismic surveys. But these are very different kinds of sound waves, and the bottom line is that in general, there's little reason to think that seismic surveys significantly harm marine mammals.

The last major argument that environmental extremists offer against drilling is that drill rigs are always going to be at risk because of hurricanes, and this could lead to large oil spills. The problem with this argument is that we have already had the ultimate test of our offshore drilling rigs when Hurricanes Katrina and Rita—both Category 5 storms when they hit the drill rigs in the Gulf of Mexico—passed through the Gulf in 2005. And the results of those storms just don't support the notion that hurricanes are a real risk for causing oil spills.

Even though about 75 percent of the rigs in the Gulf of Mexico were subjected to back-to-back Category 5 hurricanes, 89 percent of resulting oil spills was minor, and there were no major spills at all, according to official MMS figures.[7] The MMS also found no evidence of any oil reaching the shoreline or harming birds or mammals.[8] Hurricanes Katrina and Rita tested our offshore oil industry under the worst conditions—and it passed with flying colors.

There are a number of other, minor issues that extremist groups bring up when arguing against drilling, but by now it should be clear that the same story holds true for every issue: environmental extremists will oppose drilling for more American oil no matter what the facts are, what the science says, or what history shows us. That's what they do.

We don't have to choose between more energy and a clean environment. We can drill offshore in a way that allows us to have more energy and protect the environment at the same time.

THE CLEAN TRACK RECORD
OF ALASKAN DRILLING

Prudhoe Bay is a case study showing that obtaining American oil need not reap environmental destruction. The caribou at Prudhoe Bay numbered about 5,000 when drilling began in the 1970s. Today, the herd is over 30,000—an increase of more than 600 percent.[9]

At the same time, technological improvements are allowing energy companies to drill in the most environmentally sound way ever. For example, existing oil fields in Alaska have improved their techniques significantly over the past decades. Early production allowed for roughly twenty oil wells to be drilled in an area of about sixty-five acres. Today technology has advanced so far that twenty wells only occupy six to ten acres.[10]

The Department of Interior has already stated that any new development in ANWR would have to meet the strictest environmental safeguards and must only be done with the newest technology.[11] Mainstream environmentalism recognizes that we can have more American energy from ANWR without destroying the natural beauty of that sanctuary.

BREAKTHROUGHS IN OIL SHALE TECHNOLOGY

Oil shale is a great example of how new technologies allow us to have more energy and simultaneously protect the environment. For decades, the only way energy companies could extract oil from shale would have been to set up large-scale mining projects and heat the shale that had been mined. Since this technique could have been very disruptive to the environment, it presented a serious problem with the development of oil shale. In fact, a 2005 RAND study found that the most serious challenge facing oil shale development is how much the land will be disturbed.

But thanks to new technology and techniques, oil may now be recovered from shale by heating the shale underground without mining the rock. This new in-situ process is an enormous improvement over surface shale mining and promises to cause minimal environmental impact.

That same RAND study specified that in-situ would likely be "much less disruptive" to the land than surface mining. And Shell Oil's early testing of its new in-situ technology is even more environmentally friendly.[12]

Virtually all resource extraction techniques improve dramatically over time, and we can expect American ingenuity and American technology to decrease rapidly the environmental impacts of oil shale as development progresses.

THE PROMISE OF CLEAN COAL TECHNOLOGY

One of the most exciting areas for environmental protection and energy use is clean coal technology. Even though the amount of electricity produced from coal has increased by 182 percent since 1970, there has been a 42 percent drop in emissions from coal power plants during that time. And new carbon capture and storage technology promises to produce electricity from coal with almost zero carbon emissions.

As explained in Chapter 3, carbon capture and storage allows us to trap the carbon released from coal power plants and pump it into the ground before it goes into the atmosphere. With this technique, almost all the carbon would stay in the ground for over 1,000 years without seeping out. And because in the United States we have over 1,500 years of storage capacity where we could pump the carbon, we would give ourselves over a thousand years to come up with new technologies to radically cut our carbon emissions. Having read this far into this book, you should realize that this will be plenty of time given how much progress we're making right now.

We don't have to choose between using our most abundant natural resource and protecting the environment. We can use coal to provide us with the energy we need while producing virtually no carbon emissions. All it takes is a serious commitment to innovation.

PRODUCING NUCLEAR POWER WITH ENVIRONMENTAL SAFEGUARDS

Of the 104 nuclear plants ever built in America, only one has suffered a serious accident: Pennsylvania's Three Mile Island in 1979. Yet even this event caused zero environmental or health problems.

As previously discussed, the Three Mile Island accident, which was caused by the partial core meltdown of a reactor, led to years of public distrust of nuclear power. Since the health and environmental effects of the accident have often been grossly exaggerated, it's worth recounting how they're described by the U.S. Nuclear Regulatory Commission:

> Detailed studies of the radiological consequences of the accident have been conducted by the NRC, the Environmental Protection Agency, the Department of Health, Education and Welfare (now Health and Human Services), the Department of Energy, and the State of Pennsylvania. Several independent studies have also been conducted. Estimates are that the average dose to about 2 million people in the area was only about 1 millirem. To put this into context, exposure from a full set of chest x-rays is about 6 millirem. Compared

to the natural radioactive background dose of about 100-125 millirem per year for the area, the collective dose to the community from the accident was very small. The maximum dose to a person at the site boundary would have been less than 100 millirem.

In the months following the accident, although questions were raised about possible adverse effects from radiation on human, animal, and plant life in the TMI area, none could be directly correlated to the accident. Thousands of environmental samples of air, water, milk, vegetation, soil, and foodstuffs were collected by various groups monitoring the area. Very low levels of radionuclides could be attributed to releases from the accident. However, comprehensive investigations and assessments by several well-respected organizations have concluded that in spite of serious damage to the reactor, most of the radiation was contained and that the actual release had negligible effects on the physical health of individuals or the environment.[13]

Likewise, the World Nuclear Association found that the accident had no measurable health effects on the area's residents:

The TMI-2 accident caused concerns about the possibility of radiation-induced health effects, principally cancer, in the area surrounding the plant. Because of those concerns, the Pennsylvania Department of Health for 18 years maintained a registry of more than 30,000 people who lived within five miles of Three Mile Island at the time of the accident. The state's registry was discontinued in mid 1997, without any evidence of unusual health trends in the area.

Indeed, more than a dozen major, independent health studies of the accident showed no evidence of any abnormal number of cancers around TMI years after the accident. The only detectable effect was psychological stress during and shortly after the accident.[14]

The accident, according to the U.S. Nuclear Regulatory Commission, led to "permanent and sweeping changes" in nuclear power regulations to improve public safety. These, accompanied by strict oversight from the Department of Energy, have allowed nuclear power to become safer virtually every year, both for plant workers and for the environment.

We can expect that Pennsylvanians—those most directly affected by the accident—would best understand its real consequences. Thus, it's interesting to note that a July 31, 2008, poll by Quinnipiac found that most Pennsylvanians, by a margin of 58 to 32 percent, support building new nuclear power plants. A majority of Republicans and independents—72 percent and 57 percent, respectively—backed new plants, while even a plurality of Democrats supported them, with 48 percent in favor and 41 percent opposed.[15]

We can have more energy and reduce emissions at the same time once we develop more nuclear power. This is why nuclear power is one of the best examples of commonsense environmentalism. We don't have to choose between conservation and prosperity—we can have both.

CONSERVING ENERGY WITHOUT
SACRIFICING OUR WAY OF LIFE

In Chapter 1 you read examples of American and foreign corporations taking aggressive action to cut their energy use and conserve more. This not only makes sense from an environmental
standpoint, but it's also smart business because it forces companies and individuals to use energy more efficiently. This is something every mainstream environmentalist can support.

There is a big difference, however, between improving efficiency and sacrificing the American way of life. When environmental extremists lecture the public about driving SUVs, eating
meat, or using a dishwasher, they reveal how out of touch with
mainstream environmentalism they really are. A commonsense
environmental strategy doesn't condemn people for being prosperous and happy. Instead, it encourages conservation through
efficiency, innovation, and technological progress. The way to
conserve energy is to use it better, not by making Americans give
up the lifestyle they have worked so hard to secure or the modern
conveniences that improve their quality of life.

Our generation faces the extraordinary challenge of bringing
to bear science, technology, and the principles of effective markets in order to enable people to have a good life both economically and environmentally.

Four hundred years of American experience has demonstrated
that a commitment to science, entrepreneurship, and free markets can create better solutions for a better future than lawyers
and bureaucrats, with their never-ending schemes of regulation
and taxation.

It's time for a new, mainstream, and commonsense vision for environmental leadership that supports more American energy and environmental responsibility at the same time. With your help, we can create a future that is more prosperous *and* has a cleaner environment.

SIX

THE BIGGER CHALLENGE

TWO FUTURES, TWO VALUE SYSTEMS, AND TWO COALITIONS OF POWER

A lot of people will look at the facts outlined in this book and wonder why some people are so opposed to solving our energy problems by developing more American energy now to create jobs and keep American energy money in America.

They will look at our lengthy list of practical action items and think they're so obvious that it shouldn't be difficult to get Washington to adopt them.

After all, many of these proposals are supported by an overwhelming majority of Americans. Eighty-one percent of the American people support a Manhattan Project for energy, while they favor more exploration for oil and gas by a margin of three to one or better.

Yet everything seems locked up in partisan conflict.

A reasonable citizen might ask, "What's going on?"

The answer is that we are in the midst of a much bigger power struggle that involves more than just votes over drilling for oil, developing clean coal, building nuclear power plants, or any of the other positive solutions we've outlined.

What's really at stake is two very different futures for America built around two opposing value systems advocated by two coalitions of power.

Down one road is a dynamic America producing its own energy, independent of dictators, using science and technology to create an exciting future, and continuing its role as the most prosperous and technologically advanced country in the world.

Down the other road is a litigation, regulation, and taxation system of government dominance with slow growth, expensive and scarce energy, and the replacement of the United States by China and India as the world's most advanced and prosperous nations.

Thus energy is a key fight in a larger battle over the future of America.

A STARK DIFFERENCE IN VALUES

There is a historic America that believes in economic growth, promotes individual liberty, recognizes and rewards entrepreneurship, values the work ethic, and actively encourages progress. It constantly seeks out new, improved ways of doing things in order to produce a better way of life.

This America, with its belief in progress, is captured in Disney World's "Carousel of Progress," which is the most visited stage program in the country.

My grandchildren, Maggie and Robert, love watching the show. It starts in the 1890s with gas lights and ice boxes and works its way up to the present with a series of technological improvements in every generation.

The America that believes in progress is an optimistic, future-oriented country that boldly undertakes experiments and is not afraid of failing so long as you get back up and try again.

This deep sense of American uniqueness was captured in the song "I'm Proud to Be an American," which was popular when President Reagan was a proudly American president.

However, we have witnessed the gradual spread of a "post-American" ideology that stands in stark opposition to the American exceptionalism and sense of achievement that have characterized our history

This post-American value system sees entrepreneurs as dangerous, capitalism as destructive, successful businesspeople as targets of taxation and envy, the American heritage as bad, and Americans in general as inadequate people with bad attitudes and worse ideas who need to be improved, controlled, and limited.

This pessimistic ideology began to build momentum during the counterculture of the 1960s and the accompanying anti-war movement. It drew upon European and American intellectual distaste for American society, which had come to lead the world.

These left-wing intellectuals found themselves in alliance with a generation of young people who embraced reckless living and drug use as a form of rebellion against authority. Many of the youths who adhered to this ideology are today's tenured senior faculty, senior editorial writers, and media personalities.

These ideologues repudiated historic American values, and this inclination found its way into the court system. Lawyers are part of the intellectual class, and the virus of post-Americanism that infected campuses, Hollywood, and the news media soon found a friendly reception among numerous judges.

The infiltration of the courts was especially important because the Warren Court in 1958 asserted the doctrine of "judicial supremacy," which has given judges near-dictatorial powers to rewrite American laws to fit their own prejudices. For the last fifty years there has been a steady judicial assault on the historic American modes of life.

Courts have been vital to post-Americans, who clearly can't win an election based on their values. Thus they seek out like-minded lawyers who've been appointed to the bench and cooperate with them in imposing what they could never win at the ballot box. It was inevitable that they would find trial lawyers among their most enthusiastic and effective allies, for they can get rich fighting for changes that Americans would never voluntarily accept.

Because post-Americans are opposed to the historic American values of entrepreneurship, local autonomy, and individual activity, they became the allies of other forces that favor collective action and oppose individual responsibility and accountability. Thus the leadership of organized labor, which had spent years fighting for work rules to protect the inefficient as well as tenure to protect the incompetent, found its collectivist views echoed by the post-American elites. Union bosses were natural allies of the post-Americans in opposition to the achievement-oriented, incentivized, and accountability model of historic America.

Consider these differences in the two value systems:

AMERICAN EXCEPTIONALISM VALUE SYSTEM	THE POST-AMERICAN VALUE SYSTEM
American citizen	Citizen of the world
We are endowed by our Creator	We are a secular society with a legal contract
Historic traditional values are timeless and are relevant today	The world requires modern, secular, and relativist values
English should be the nation's official language	Americans should speak many languages; it's "embarrassing" when ignorant Americans go overseas
Values entrepreneurs and engineers	Values bureaucrats and lawyers
Science and technology improve life and deserve investment	Science and technology are dangerous and must be controlled
Practical agreements for action	Litigation
Businesses are vital for the economy	Trial lawyers are vital for the economy
Solving problems	Refusing to change rules and regulations even if they don't work
Individual opportunity and responsibility	Collective behavior policed by government

AMERICAN EXCEPTIONALISM VALUE SYSTEM	THE POST-AMERICAN VALUE SYSTEM
More energy	Less energy
Freedom to choose your way of life and how you spend your money	Government rules force limited choices of cars, homes, etc.
Science and technology are key to solving problems	Politicians and bureaucrats are key to solving problems
Vast American resources	Resources pollute, so avoid using them
Lower taxes	Higher taxes
Individuals make their own choices	Bureaucracy is smarter than the people
Entrepreneurs invest better than bureaucrats	Government invests better than entrepreneurs
Power at home is better than power in Washington	Power in Washington is necessary to control and correct ignorant or inadequate citizens
Learning matters	The school bureaucracy matters
Merit pay and incentives for better teaching and more learning	A lockstep, one-salary scale system for everyone with no standards
Individual right to vote in secret before joining a union	Unions can organize without a vote
American national security is vital and American interests deserve strong advocacy	The world is bigger than America and we should subordinate American interests to the international good

These different value systems lead to two almost diametrically opposed coalitions that represent clashing interests.

The coalition of post-Americans, trial lawyers, the news media, big labor, the government bureaucracy, and Hollywood finds itself on one side. The historic American entrepreneurial coalition is on the other.

An abiding characteristic of the post-American coalition is the vehemence with which it attacks anyone, even its own allies, who opposes any part of its agenda. Democratic senator Zell Miller discovered this tendency first-hand a few years ago, and he ended up speaking at the 2004 Republican convention. Likewise, former Democratic senator Joseph Lieberman found himself isolated and attacked by this coalition, and survived only as an independent after losing the Democratic primary to a hard-left opponent.

President Reagan surmounted this problem by offering a program so popular and so powerful that about a third of the Democratic Party voted for his agenda and against its own allies.

In my own time in Congress we overcame the post-Americans with the Contract with America, which proposed a program of such sweeping reform that we replaced their coalition as the majority in the House of Representatives for the first time in forty years.

Then we carefully focused on big changes that the American people overwhelmingly supported. In the case of welfare reform, we actually split the Democratic Party right down the middle, with 101 Democratic congressmen voting for reform and 101 against it.

The challenge for us today is to develop a popular wave of support like there was for President Reagan and for the Contract with

America. This energy needs to be focused on developing more American energy now at lower prices and with more conservation. With that kind of support, we could forge a new bipartisan (or tripartisan, if we include independents) majority in favor of commonsense energy solutions.* Alternatively, we could attract enough individual members on an issue by issue basis to develop an ad hoc majority coalition that approves one energy measure after another.

Our immediate task is to inform and persuade the American people so they decisively repudiate the post-American coalition and insist on the policies of the pro-energy camp. This is an absolutely crucial step toward ending the energy crisis once and for all.

---

*The Platform of the American People, available at www.AmericanSolutions.com, is aimed at forming precisely this kind of tripartisan majority.

SEVEN

WHAT YOU CAN DO

A CITIZENS' ACTION PLAN

Never underestimate the intelligence of the American people nor overestimate the amount of information they have.

—JOSEPH NAPOLITAN, DEMOCRATIC CONSULTANT

For America truly to realize its energy potential, we must change our energy policy. Americans for decades have been without a strategic, comprehensive plan to boost energy production, even though much of our national security, economic prosperity, standard of living, and even our very safety depends upon reliable, affordable energy.

Think of everything you've done just today for which you relied on energy: the car or bus or train you took to work, the lights you need to see, your entertainment, your computer devices, your refrigerator, heat, air conditioning, the list goes on and on. Add traffic lights, airports, office buildings, public services, and schools, and you begin to understand just how much we depend upon affordable energy.

Now imagine that you suddenly couldn't afford all this energy, and were forced to choose what to use and what not to use. Would you cancel your vacation? Take fewer trips to see your children or grandchildren? Could you still do your job? Could you feed your family? Many Americans may soon face these stark choices, all because the politicians in Washington refuse to approve pro-energy policies.

But it's not too late. In 1994, Americans were fed up with their out-of-touch leadership in Washington, and by large numbers the people fired them.

After all, in our form of government, "we the people" have the ultimate power because it's "we the voter" who decides who gets to stay in power.

And it's time to decide. Securing safe, affordable, reliable energy is simply too important a task to be left for the next Congress to resolve.

To change America for a brighter energy future, we must act, and act now.

I know how to make Congress pay attention. I've seen the American people get their attention before. But time is critical.

We have to convince a lot of our fellow citizens that their leadership on this issue matters. We can't hope to change our energy future with citizens who just passively complain—that won't win our future. To win we must fight by engaging the process, and we can do this by asserting to Congress that we're in charge.

We are committed to taking advantage of all the resources in America that God has given us. From vast reserves of coal, to oil shale located in the Green River Basin in the West, to nuclear power, to oil and natural gas off our coasts and in Alaska.

We must communicate that there's no more time for vacillating. We want action from our leaders and we want it now. Otherwise, we'll get new leaders who will act.

The interest groups, bureaucracies, and ideologies of the last generation have had their chance for decades, and it's their failure that has landed us where we are now. Think about it. We are the greatest country in the history of mankind. Let me repeat that. We are the greatest country of all time, but we've allowed a small, anti-energy elite to effectively deny us the use of our very own energy resources. They have said "no" over and over in the name of ideological abstractions. They tell us that we're simply supposed to shut up and make do with whatever limited amount of energy they decide we should have.

Well, it's time to fight back. We Americans have a long tradition of continually expanding our prosperity, creativity, and environmental stewardship, and there's no reason why we should allow a small group of anti-energy extremists to bring this tradition to an end.

The anti-energy elites face a major obstacle in carrying out their vision for America. While they may prefer decay, and while they may want to protect their special interests deals in Washington, they're confronted by an overwhelming force—American public opinion.

We are Americans. When we decide as a people to act, no extremists, no dictator, no terrorist, no special interests, and certainly no politician will get in our way.

Only we, the American people, can insist on the change in politics and government necessary to produce a comprehensive energy plan that starts to create more American energy now while still protecting the environment.

To fix our energy policy, we really need to do just one simple yet extraordinary thing: force our government to act on the facts and evidence in the energy debate and adopt practical, commonsense solutions. It sounds obvious, yet that's exactly what the government is refusing to do now.

That will mean electing leaders—everyone from presidents and governors, to congressional representatives and senators, to state legislators, police chiefs and school board members—who share our values and our commitment to more American energy now. But above all else, it will mean that all of us, we the people, need to become leaders in the fight to change our energy policies.

CITIZEN LEADERSHIP IN THE FIGHT FOR MORE AMERICAN ENERGY

The choice we face is stark: accept the failures in government energy policy we see every week when we fill up our gas tanks, or work to change things. And change requires new, grassroots leaders, because the forces of the anti-energy status quo are not going to provide leadership on this issue.

Therefore, as I wrote in my book *Real Change*, if we are to change our country, we have to accept the challenge of leadership.

Leadership can be exercised at whatever level interests you, and to whatever degree you're willing to devote your time and energy to saving your community and your country.

It all begins with values and vision. We value a future where we don't worry about unstable dictators turning on and off our energy supplies.

We share the common values of access, affordability, reliability, safety, and health for us and our environment. Our vision is more American energy at lower cost that helps our economy grow, reduces our dependence on foreign sources of oil and protects our environment.

We intend to bring about this future as quickly as possible. Waiting a decade to begin realizing our vision is unacceptable. We need changes now to allow us to harness our true energy potential as quickly as possible.

The anti-energy elites, in contrast, have advocated a do-nothing strategy that accepts higher prices and less energy. They want to punish Americans into driving less and driving smaller cars. They want to force Americans into living in smaller homes in urban areas, even if we don't want to.

This shortsighted approach of inducing pain on the American people has now hardened into the current entrenched bureaucratic government and clichéd thinking among the anti-energy elitists. We have a lot of work to do to turn it around, and it will require all of us to take power back from the system and demand dramatic, transformational change.

Any citizen leader who thinks we can get more American energy now and reduce our dependence on foreign countries without dramatically different policies is kidding himself. He should turn to the thinking of Albert Einstein for leadership advice.

Einstein had a firm rule for developing new solutions to complex problems. According to him, we begin by realizing this:

thinking that doing more of the same will lead to a different outcome is a sign of insanity.

When we fight for change in our energy policy, we need to remember the Einstein principle. When people tell you failure is acceptable and that you should be patient while the current system continues to founder and energy prices continue to rise, cheerfully tell them that thinking that doing more of the same will lead to a different outcome is a sign of insanity. But you prefer to behave sanely and focus on real change.

THE PROSPECT FOR REAL CHANGE IN AMERICA'S ENERGY POLICY

To solve the energy crisis, we need a citizens' movement dedicated to changing our laws.

I helped found American Solutions for Winning the Future to develop solutions, advocate real change, and train and empower citizens and elected officials to be more effective across the country. If you go to www.AmericanSolutions.com, you can see all the many developments, including the Platform of the American People that we produced last fall to offer the country a red-white-and-blue program to replace the red-versus-blue partisan split.

You can read the entire Platform of the American People at www.AmericanSolutions.com/Platform. And you can read the specific planks that outline our pro-energy and pro-environment approach in Appendix 1 of this book.

American Solutions is focused on educating, mobilizing, encouraging, and empowering citizens across a broad range of issues, but it's not an attempt to organize or direct in a centralized fashion. We at American Solutions believe it's important to develop solutions at the local level through local leadership.

It's precisely because of the unique mission of American Solutions that we have tried in this book to give you the information you need to rise above partisan politics and be a leader in your community for more American energy now.

We need millions of citizen leaders who are going to win the argument that America needs a new, comprehensive energy policy that focuses on lowering gas and diesel prices through expanded oil and gas production, more nuclear power, more clean coal, more biofuels, and more wind—and in the long-term on developing new energy sources.

Your leadership is crucial to protecting America's vital interests. Our nation's national security is currently at risk because of our dependence on foreign oil from countries that are hostile to America and American interests. In many ways, by importing so much oil from the Middle East, we are funding some of the very countries that threaten us and our allies.

Similarly, America's economic security is threatened by the soaring price of gasoline and diesel fuel. Truck companies are going out of business. Police departments are cutting back on patrols. Small businesses are laying off workers. And hardworking American families are struggling to pay for rising food costs.

We need a new generation of leaders to rise up to do what Americans have historically done: overcome our challenges and lead the way to a safer and more prosperous America.

FIRST STEP TOWARD WINNING THE ENERGY DEBATE: THE "DRILL HERE, DRILL NOW, PAY LESS" MOVEMENT

We faced a serious challenge to our prosperity early in 2008. Amidst growing public concern over the increasing price at the pump, the U.S. Senate did the unthinkable: it introduced the Boxer-Warner-Lieberman climate change bill that would have added $1 per gallon to the price of gasoline.

At that time I knew it was imperative to mobilize the American people in opposition to this disastrous bill. As a result, we launched at American Solutions the "Drill Here, Drill Now, Pay Less" petition.

The petition's message was clear and concise: we need an energy policy that produces more American energy, not restricts it. And we need an energy policy that lowers the price of gasoline and diesel, not increases it.

Soon after we began the petition, the Boxer-Warner-Lieberman bill was defeated, and our momentum continued to grow for more American energy now. In just a few weeks, American Solutions gathered 1 million signatures and was widely credited with igniting the national focus on more domestic drilling.

As the petition drive expanded into a nationwide movement, we heard from thousands of struggling Americans who are frustrated by Congress's inaction. By signing the petition, more than 1.4 million Democrats, Republicans, and independents have appealed to Congress to allow environmentally responsible ways to produce more energy here at home.

They did not call for higher taxes on oil companies.

They did not blame foreigners for our energy problems.

They did not beg the Saudis to sell us more oil.

And so their message to the Congress was this: "The American people have spoken. Are you listening?"

It doesn't seem that Congress has gotten the message yet. But other key leaders have.

A great example of this occurred over summer 2008 when President Bush repealed an 18-year-old executive order put in place by his father that prohibited offshore oil drilling. Notably, the president's repeal occurred just seven weeks after American Solutions launched the "Drill Here, Drill Now, Pay Less" petition drive. This shows that if the American people demand real change in our energy policies, we can achieve it.

With President Bush having lifted the executive ban on offshore drilling, Congress has now run out of excuses not to follow suit. Congress should immediately remove its own offshore drilling ban, which is now the main obstacle preventing us from reaping the many benefits of offshore oil drilling.

Now is the time to tell Congress you want action, not words. The most effective message you can send to anyone who wants to represent us in Washington is this: get the job done NOW.

As usual, the American people know intuitively what Washington just doesn't understand: It's not just Republicans who are struggling to put gas in their cars. Democratic and independent families, commuters, and small business owners are hurting, too.

When they come and ask for your vote, ask for their action.

DO IT FOR AMERICA

The lesson of World War II is that when America is facing a crisis we should drown our opponents and competitors in our productive capabilities.

But that's not the only lesson.

We should do it all and do it now, but we should also do it for America.

It's important to remember that there's a patriotic drive and determination behind our energy policy vision. The campaign for a twenty-first-century secure energy program is about lowering gas prices, but it's also about something bigger.

It's about protecting America by cutting off the flow of our dollars to the foreign dictators that control much of our oil supply.

It's about coming together and flexing our national muscles to make life better.

It's about honoring the sacrifice of our parents and grandparents by giving our children and grandchildren a better America than the one we inherited.

America's ready to stop talking and take action. Isn't it time Washington got the message?

DRILLING IS JUST THE BEGINNING

We do not believe that drilling is the final answer to our energy problems. On the contrary, it's the indispensable beginning.

We recognize that there are 240 million cars and trucks in the current fleet and that we need to take steps in the short run to bring down the price of gas for working and retired Americans.

We recognize that the airlines are under enormous financial stress, and we need to bring down the cost of aviation fuel to save the jobs of airline employees and protect the budgets of airline travelers.

We recognize that truckers are being devastated by the rise in diesel fuel prices, and we could soon face a crisis of effective transportation as truckers go broke. This could be accompanied by a big jump in inflation as energy prices are passed on to the consumer in every form.

We also recognize that the skyrocketing price of natural gas has been driving American chemical industry and manufacturing jobs offshore.

Just as we need a comprehensive long-term strategy, we also need immediate steps to provide relief to the American people. These begin with drilling.

TOP TEN THINGS YOU CAN DO NOW TO WIN THE ENERGY DEBATE

We won't be able to change our energy policy and provide short-term relief at the pump until we win the energy debate.

As Margaret Thatcher once said, "First you win the argument; then you win the vote." In American public life, winning the argument is the first step toward fundamentally changing public policy. And this book is meant to equip the reader with the facts necessary to win the argument for more American energy.

A large part of winning the argument is presenting the facts in a patiently persuasive manner. Since you now have the facts on your side, there is no need to be confrontational. Most people distrust stridency, but will listen to a cheerfully presented, logically constructed set of facts.

Equipped with the facts, it's up to you, the citizen leader, to communicate them to your community and elected officials. Here are a few practical steps you can take:

1. **Ask your congressional representatives, U.S. senators, and state leaders to sign the "More American Energy Now 'First Steps' Pledge."** In Appendix 4, you'll find the "More American Energy Now 'First Steps' Pledge." By asking your U.S. Senators, local congressional representative, and local state legislators to sign it, you'll find out where each of them stands on the urgent issue of developing more American energy. The pledge outlines the first three steps that America should take to lower energy prices now and set us on the path to greater energy independence:

   ● End the federal ban on offshore drilling for oil and natural gas, and give coastal states the right to choose whether to begin drilling off their shores

   ● End the federal ban on drilling for oil and natural gas in the Alaskan National Wildlife Refuge (ANWR)

   ● End all prohibitions on the development of the more than 800 billion barrels of oil shale in Colorado, Utah, Wyoming, and the rest of the United States.

Get them to sign it now, and get them to do it now.

2.   **Sign the petition**. Let your voice be heard by signing—and urging your friends and family to sign—the "Drill Here, Drill Now, Pay Less" petition at www.AmericanSolutions.com, which reads:

> We, therefore, the undersigned citizens of the United States, petition the U.S. Congress to act immediately to lower gasoline prices (and diesel and other fuel prices) by authorizing the exploration of proven energy resources to reduce our dependance on foreign energy sources from unstable countries.

Remember, it's the right of every American citizen to petition the government for change. Believe me, when millions of people sign a single petition, you can bet Washington will pay attention. It already is, and you can see it playing out in the presidential campaign. The petition is effective, so sign it today. At the back of this book you'll find your very own membership card that you can tear out and carry with you to show your friends your membership in the American Coalition for More American Energy Now.

3.   **Call your congressman and local officials.** That is what they're there for. They represent you, so make

them work for you. Tell them you signed the petition and ask if they support pro-American or post-American energy policies. Tell them that over 1.4 million Americans of all political backgrounds have also signed the petition, and their job as an elected official is to listen to the will of the American people. Ask them to sign the "First Steps" pledge.

4. **Know the issues, facts, and arguments.** Commit to learning all you can about America's need for a national strategic energy policy and how important it is to our safety, economy, national security, and way of life. Read every article you can. Subscribe to Google Alerts using key words to let you know when something new is written on the issue. Track the progress of the debate. Make sure you see the new movie *We Have the Power* at www.WeHaveThePowerMovie.com. Become an expert. See Appendix 2 at the back of this book for key facts on the energy debate, and see Appendix 3 to learn rebuttals to the most common arguments against more American energy now.

    As the energy debate evolves and the anti-energy elites devise new excuses not to produce more American-made energy, make sure you stay current with the newest developments. You can find an up-to-date list of facts and arguments at AmericanSolutions.com. If you encounter a new argument you can't answer, write me at: newt@americansolutions.com, and we will add that to the "Solutions and

Answers" section. You can also go to www.American-
Solutions.com/EnergyHandbook to download public opinion research and short reports on energy, the
environment, and technological innovation.

5. **Write an op-ed or a letter to the editor.** Writing an
article for your local newspaper is another easy way
to inform others about the importance of Ameri-
can-made energy. Most people still get a lot of their
information from newspapers, so it's essential to
win the battle of ideas in this arena. The letter can
be short, but it should be fact-based and focused on
one topic. If you see something in your paper that is
worth correcting or encouraging, send a letter. If it
appears on a weblog, post a response. Stay on topic
and stick to the facts. The truth will win out.

6. **Call your local talk radio show.** Similar to local
newspapers, many people get information from
local talk radio shows. Calling in to your local radio
show only takes a few minutes, and your voice will
often reach thousands of listeners at a time. If your
radio host believes, as you do, in the need for more
American energy now, suggest they do a daily seg-
ment on gas prices until Congress takes meaningful action that includes both short-term and
long-term solutions.

Talk radio is one of the most effective ways to
communicate. Mostly you will be talking to someone while they listen in their car, so stay calm—you
wouldn't yell at someone sitting next to you in your

car, would you? Stick to the facts. You can use the same language we've used in this book. Remember, you want to persuade.

7. **Share what you learn with friends.** In this age of technology, perhaps the most integral tool to winning the argument is the Internet. Through the use of blogs, forwarding emails to friends, the Solutions Lab at www.AmericanSolutions.com, video sharing websites like YouTube, and social networking websites like Facebook, the "Drill Here, Drill Now, Pay Less" petition spread virally on the Internet faster than we ever expected. Share what you learn with others. Become a leader on the issue. People will begin to look to you for information, and that's when you become a champion on this issue. Urge them to read this book and others that advocate the pro-energy position. Remember, millions of Americans depend on us to win this argument for our future.

8. **Be creative.** If you are feeling creative or you have natural artistic ability, do something artistic that will capture the spirit and the imagination of this movement. Write a slogan, a song, or maybe a poem. Paint a picture or do some graphics works. Make a sign. Display your "Drill Here, Drill Now" bumper sticker. How about a PowerPoint presentation or a short movie?

9. **Tell your story.** The good news is that all these tools are readily at your disposal. The most powerful way

to persuade others is to tell your story of how soaring gas, diesel, and other fuel prices are affecting your life. To do this, tape a short video that tells your story and post it on YouTube. After you finish the video, email it to your friends and family, and encourage them to create a similar video. People will connect with real life stories of Americans struggling because of high fuel prices. Whatever you think can get attention, go for it.

10. **Start a group.** Finally, starting a group of like-minded activists is a great way to generate additional ideas and organize these activities to have the maximum possible impact. At American Solutions, we've created a Real Change Chapter program to help you organize interested citizens in your community who are committed to winning the energy debate. We'll send you a weekly e-newsletter so you can stay informed on the latest news and receive the resources you need to build a successful group. You can find out more information about the Real Change chapters at www.AmericanSolutions.com/RealChange.

This list is by no means exhaustive. Be inventive. Be creative. But most of all, be persuasive and cheerfully persistent.

I am confident that we can have a better energy future because I know millions of Americans will accept no less and will act to change things. You can be a leader helping to make it happen.

Remember, we have the power to give America power.

"DRILL HERE, DRILL NOW. I AM ALL OVER THAT!"

You know you've hit a nerve when strangers in foreign countries repeat your slogans back to you. During the peak of high energy prices back home, my wife Calista and I were in Gdansk, Poland to shoot a film about Ronald Reagan. We were standing in front of the Solidarity Gate of the Lenin shipyards when three Americans approached us. One said, "Drill here, drill now. I am all over that!"

For me, it was a moment of clarity. There, on the site where the movement first began that ultimately overthrew Polish communism and inspired a fellow captive nation to bring down the Berlin Wall, another citizens' movement was revealing its strength.

As I wrote in Chapter 1, this book is about a people who are in pain and a government that's in denial.

It's about a nation that was built on optimism and ingenuity, and a ruling elite that is mired in bureaucracy and defeatism.

It's about the common sense of Americans and the complacency of our leaders.

I've heard from too many Americans who are suffering because of high energy prices caused not by any iron law of economics, but by bad government policies. I've heard from too many distressed people to believe that Congress and the president aren't hearing from these Americans as well.

"THE WORST THING IS BEING AWAY FROM MY FAMILY DURING THE WEEK."

Ramona Talbert is one of the many people struggling to cope with high gas prices. She wrote me this simple, powerful note—a message that expresses better than I ever could the bind in which so many Americans find themselves:

> I live in rural Tennessee. I drive an hour to work at a college campus, so I work for the state, which means I am very low paid. My husband is retired and he gets Medicare. I make $19,300 a year. My gas bill got so large that I had to make other plans. I usually charge my gas all month and pay it off at the end of the month, but I could no longer get it paid each month. So I moved to a small apartment on campus because it was so much cheaper than driving back and forth to work 90 miles. I drive a small car, a PT Cruiser, but I have to go up and down a steep mountain road. I was spending over $400 a month on gas. This apartment is only $320 a month and

that includes all bills except electric, which has so far been under $50 a month. The worst thing is being away from my family during the week. I only go home on weekends.

The most tragic thing about stories like Ramona's is that they're entirely preventable. As I have argued in this book, we have the resources and the capability to stop this from happening. The American people know this, even if our leaders don't.

When we approached people on the street for a video for American Solutions, we told them that America has areas that are rich in oil and other resources that our government won't allow us to recover—even as gas prices go through the roof and our energy dollars flow to foreign dictatorships. The facts we outlined included the following:

- America has at least an estimated 800 billion barrels of shale oil in Colorado, Wyoming, and Utah that could be developed. Congress won't allow it.
- America has an estimated 18.92 billion barrels of oil and 85.7 trillion cubic feet of natural gas off our shores that could be extracted in an environmentally safe manner. Congress won't allow it.
- America has an estimated 10.4 billion barrels of petroleum in the Arctic National Wildlife Refuge that could be developed. Congress won't allow it.
- Cuba, which recently entered into a drilling agreement with China, can drill for oil within sixty miles of the Florida coast. Congress won't allow American companies to do that.

We received a range of reactions. Some people already familiar with these upsetting facts simply shook their heads in dismay. Others, upon hearing of this state of affairs for the first time, were outraged.

Distilled, their reactions eventually became our rallying cry: Drill Here. Drill Now. Pay Less.

For the people it's a no-brainer. For our governing elites, it's just "no."

ECONOMICS 101 VS. THE
ANTI-ENERGY ELITES

When it comes to making America energy independent, the willful blindness of our anti-energy elites even extends to basic questions of economics.

One of their main talking points against allowing drilling offshore or in ANWR, for instance, is that it won't have any impact on today's energy prices. To Americans now struggling to put fuel in their tanks, the elites say developing new energy sources won't offer any relief.

But the story of two economists who disagreed with this claim shows how false and misleading this argument really is.

The two economics professors conducted a study to examine what the impact of opening up ANWR would be on today's oil prices. Their conclusions speak for themselves: "We find that oil that is expected to reach the market some years hence has an immediate impact on oil prices." Furthermore, "If oil firms were allowed to drill in ANWR and many of the other areas that are currently off limits to oil production, it is possible that these areas together might have a significant impact on world oil prices."

But when the professors submitted their findings to be published in *The Energy Journal,* a prestigious economics publication, they were rejected—not because the editors disagreed with their conclusion that developing ANWR would lower energy prices, but because the editors thought their conclusion was so obvious and well-known that it didn't merit publication.

Here's what the editors' rejection letter said: "Basically, your main result (the present impact of an anticipated future supply change) is already known to economists (although perhaps not to the Democratic Policy Committee)."

Who can argue otherwise?

AN ARGUMENT BEGINNING WITH ENERGY AND ENDING WITH AMERICA'S FUTURE

With this book, I've tried to give you the facts you need—the facts we all need—to win the argument over America's energy future.

This argument begins with the environmentally responsible development of America's existing energy resources. But it doesn't end there.

It continues with developing alternative energies—wind, solar, biofuels, and others—to achieve sustainable energy independence. But the argument doesn't end there either.

In the end, the argument put forward in this book is an argument about America. It's a call for us all to take a more active role in shaping what kind of country we will leave our children and grandchildren.

Do we want to leave a country that strangles itself in bureaucracy, regulation and litigation, or an America that liberates itself with entrepreneurialism, innovation, and creation?

A country that hands its fortune and its future over to foreign dictators, or an America that takes charge of its own security and wins its own future?

A country ruled by the malaise of Jimmy Carter, or an America freed by the optimism of Ronald Reagan?

The argument over our energy future embodies all these choices. And from ordinary Americans on the streets of our cities and towns to the American visitors at Solidarity Gate, we know on which side we stand.

All that's left is to let our leaders know that the American people have already chosen.

PLATFORM OF THE AMERICAN PEOPLE

The two political parties can find many issues about which to disagree. It would be a healthy change if they could begin by recognizing the values and concerns of the vast majority of Americans and jointly agree to a core platform that could bring us together before turning to divisive issues.

Everything in this platform has the support of a majority of Republicans, a majority of Democrats, and a majority of independents. We call these unifying issues the Platform of the American People. Our hope is that beginning with local conventions and up through district, state, and the national conventions, both political parties will consider adopting this platform as a foundation.

Imagine how much healthier America would be if by January 2009 both parties were committed to adopting a series of issues the American people favor by large majorities. If you would like to work to get your party to adopt the Platform of the American People, please go to www.AmericanSolutions.com/Platform and sign up. You can also discover others in your community who have agreed to work on common goals for America.

ENERGY: OIL, COAL, NUCLEAR, AND NATIONAL SECURITY*

- We want our elected leaders in Washington to focus on increasing the energy supplies of the United States and lowering the costs of gasoline and electricity.
- To combat the rising cost of energy and reduce our dependence on foreign energy sources, we support the United States using more of its own domestic energy resources, including the oil and coal it already has here in the U.S.
- Our current dependence on foreign oil threatens our national security by making us vulnerable to dangerous dictatorships.
- We should build more oil refineries in America to lower the cost of gas and reduce our dependence on foreign oil.

---

* These are the platform's energy and environment planks. The entire Platform of the American People can be found at www.AmericanSolutions.com.

ENVIRONMENT

- We have an obligation to be good stewards of God's creation for future generations.
- We can have a healthy economy and a healthy environment.
- We can solve our environmental problems faster and cheaper with innovation and new technology than with more litigation and more government regulation.
- Entrepreneurs are more likely to solve America's energy and environmental problems than bureaucrats.
- If we use technology and innovation and incentives we do not need to raise taxes to clean up our environment.
- We support giving tax credits to companies that cut carbon emissions as an incentive to cut pollution.
- We want to encourage businesses to voluntarily cut pollution and give them financial incentives to do this but, if necessary, we will require them to do so.
- We should give tax credits to homeowners and builders who incorporate alternative energy systems in their homes, like solar, wind, and geothermal energy.
- We support offering tax credits for people who turn in older, high-polluting cars.
- Climate change and global warming are probably happening.
- We support building more nuclear power plants to cut carbon emissions.

- We should hold city governments to the same standards for cleaning waste water as are applied to private industry.
- We are prepared to use public funds to preserve green space and parks to protect natural areas from development but especially with public and private partnerships.
- We favor property tax credits to private landowners who agree not to develop their land and agree not to sell it to developers.

KEY FACTS ABOUT AMERICA'S ENERGY RESOURCES

FUTURE ENERGY NEEDS

- The United States will need about 18 percent more energy by the year 2030.
- It is projected that the world will need 50 percent more energy by the year 2030.

OIL PRODUCTION AND PRICES

- Increasing American oil production by 1 million barrels per day would reduce our future dependence on foreign oil by 7.5 percent.

- Increasing American oil production by 1 million barrels per day would provide 20 percent more American oil over the next forty years.
- In 1970, the U.S. produced 10 million barrels of oil per day. Today, America only produces 5.1 million barrels per day.
- The U.S. spends $700 billion each year on foreign oil imports.
- The increase in the price of a barrel of oil from $80 to $100 was the equivalent of a $150 billion tax hike on American families.

OIL AND NATURAL GAS RESOURCES PLACED OFF-LIMITS BY CONGRESS

OFFSHORE

- About 85 percent of the Outer Continental Shelf off the shores of the continental United States is off-limits to development.
- U.S. law prohibits the development of approximately 19 billion barrels of undeveloped oil resources offshore.
- U.S. law prohibits the development of approximately 85.7 trillion cubic feet of undeveloped natural gas resources offshore.

ONSHORE

- U.S. laws and regulations prohibit the development of approximately 19 billion barrels of undeveloped oil resources onshore.
- U.S. laws and regulations prohibit the development of approximately 94.5 trillion cubic feet of undeveloped natural gas resources onshore.

ALASKA NATIONAL WILDLIFE REFUGE (ANWR)

- U.S. law prohibits the development of approximately 10.4 billion barrels of undeveloped oil resources in ANWR.
- Obtaining the oil in ANWR would require drilling on less than one-half of 1 percent of the acreage of the refuge.
- Drilling in ANWR would create as many as 130,000 new jobs.

RESERVE GROWTH

- When drilling first began in Alaska's Prudhoe Bay, it was estimated that there were 9 billion barrels of oil in the ground. As of today, 15 billion barrels of oil have been discovered there.
- In 1984, the Minerals Management Service estimated there were 6 billion barrels of oil and 60 trillion cubic feet of natural gas in the Gulf of Mexico. As of today,

we have discovered 13 billion barrels of oil and 152 trillion cubic feet of natural gas in the Gulf.

OIL SHALE

- There are approximately 800 billion barrels of oil in the form of oil shale located in Colorado, Utah, and Wyoming. These resources are estimated to be at least three times the proven oil reserves of Saudi Arabia.
- Congress has made it illegal to develop most of this oil shale.
- Shell estimates its new technique of extracting oil from shale will allow the oil to remain economically competitive even if crude oil prices fall as low as $25 per barrel.

OIL REFINERIES

- Largely due to excessive regulations, the United States has not built a new refinery since 1976.

COAL

- About 27 percent of the world's coal supply is in the United States.
- There is enough coal in the United States to supply America with energy for 250 years.
- There is twice as much coal in the United States as there is in China.

NUCLEAR POWER

America has not licensed a new nuclear power plant since 1979. Since then, Japan has constructed thirty-six new plants and has eleven more under development, while France has built fifty-six plants.

- America gets about 20 percent of its electricity from nuclear power, compared to 33 percent in Japan and 71 percent in France.
- If the United States got the same percentage of its electricity from nuclear power as France does, we would emit 2.2 billion fewer tons of carbon dioxide in the atmosphere each year. This would exceed the targets set in the Kyoto Protocol by 15 percent.

REBUTTING THE CRITICS OF MORE AMERICAN ENERGY NOW

The unnecessary energy crisis caused by our government can only be ended by you. After reading this book, you now know how we got into this mess and how to solve it, but it's up to you to write letters to your local newspaper, call in to radio shows, call your congressman or senator, or do any number of other things that will build momentum and pressure for real change in America's energy policy so we can develop more American energy now.

This appendix will give you some of the key arguments and rebuttals you can use to help win the debate that will lead to more American energy now, lower prices, reduced dependence on foreign countries, and a cleaner environment.

Because the arguments of the anti-energy coalition are shifting so rapidly, and new and stranger arguments are being invented all the time, you can keep up to date on the debate by visiting www.AmericanSolutions.com

ARGUMENT AGAINST MORE AMERICAN ENERGY NOW

Everyone knows drilling will not provide any short-term relief in the price of oil because it will take many years before new drilling will lead to new supplies.

REBUTTAL

First, opening up large areas offshore, in Alaska, and in other places to drilling will almost certainly have an immediate impact in lowering prices at the pump. Martin Feldstein, former chairman of the President's Council of Economic Advisers, explained in a July 1, 2008 *Wall Street Journal* editorial that if we increase the amount of oil we will have in the future—which would happen if Congress lifted the moratorium on offshore and oil shale drilling and made onshore drilling easier—oil's future value will diminish, and this lowers prices today.

Why? Imagine you're an oil producer. You're making a lot of money right now because there's a limited supply of oil, which means people are willing to pay more for the oil you produce. But what happens if you find out that there will be a lot more oil available in the future because the U.S. will start drilling for more of it? You know that people won't be willing to pay as much for your oil because there will be more oil available to meet their needs. So what do you do? You try to sell more oil now, when there is less supply and prices are higher. But because all the other oil producers have the same idea, the result is that there's an overall increase in supply of oil around the world—which lowers prices now.

The bottom line is this: opening up new oil and gas fields in the U.S. for development, even if new supplies will not actually reach our gas tank for several years, will lower prices today.

Second, the argument that we should not pursue energy strategies if they take a long time to develop is really an argument against developing almost all forms of energy. Does this mean we pursue long-term alternative energy solutions like wind, solar, and hydrogen because these will all take a long time to develop? For example, it will take years before hydrogen fuel cells and electric cars will be able to decrease our use of oil. Likewise, new nuclear power plants will take years to build and so will new refineries.

This argument has been made by opponents of oil drilling for the last thirty years. In the case of ANWR, Congress passed a bill in 1995 to open up drilling there, but the measure was vetoed by President Clinton. It is now thirteen years since that veto. If we had only acted earlier, we would have billions of barrels of more American oil today and significantly lower prices.

ARGUMENT AGAINST MORE AMERICAN ENERGY NOW

The U.S. only has a small percentage (2 to 6 percent) of the world's oil supply, and since oil is a global commodity, our increased production will not affect prices much.

REBUTTAL

First, the estimate that the U.S. has two to six percent of the world's oil supply does not hold up to scrutiny.

In oil shale alone, found in the Green River Formation in parts of Utah, Colorado, and Wyoming, the U.S. has at least 800 billion barrels of recoverable oil, over three times the proven reserves of Saudi Arabia. This comes from a midpoint estimate in a 2005 RAND study done at the request of the Department of Energy. A higher-end estimate puts the number at over 1 trillion barrels.

Second, there are vast areas of the United States and its Outer Continental Shelf (OCS) where it's illegal to even look for oil. So it's entirely possible (or even probable) that the current estimates of our oil reserves are too low.

For example, when we first started drilling in Prudhoe Bay in Alaska, the estimates were that 9 billion barrels of oil were in the ground. Fifteen billion barrels later, we're still drilling. Similarly, in 1984 the Minerals Management Service (MMS) estimated there were 6 billion barrels of oil and 60 trillion cubic feet of natural gas in the Gulf of Mexcio. Thirteen billion barrels of oil and 152 trillion cubic feet of natural gas later, we're still getting oil and gas out of the Gulf.

We really don't know how much oil we have until we begin more comprehensive exploring.

ARGUMENT AGAINST MORE AMERICAN ENERGY NOW

We do not have enough oil in ANWR or the OCS to make any significant difference in reducing our dependence on foreign oil.

Isn't it true that the oil in ANWR, for example, would only be enough to meet American energy needs for less than a year?

REBUTTAL

This argument uses a clever technique in which the billions of barrels of oil recoverable from ANWR or the OCS are compared to how much oil Americans consume every day. The amount of reserve oil is then divided by the amount of daily consumption to see how many days of oil are contained in the reserve.

This argument is totally unrealistic. No one is claiming that the U.S. could quickly switch over to using only domestic sources of oil. We're nowhere near being able to either produce or refine that much.

The oil in these reserves would be used slowly and incrementally to replace some of the foreign oil we import. This means the oil would last us much longer than the short timeframes given by drilling opponents. As you learned in Chapter 3, producing just 1 million more barrels per day from the Pacific and Atlantic areas would provide 20 percent more domestic oil for the next four decades compared to current production.

ARGUMENT AGAINST MORE AMERICAN ENERGY NOW

Oil companies currently have access to 68 million acres of leased public lands that contain large amounts of economically recoverable oil. Drilling in these areas could generate 4.8 million barrels a day, so opening up more land to drilling is unnecessary.

REBUTTAL

The way people come up with the estimate of 4.8 million barrels is by assuming that all the acres that haven't been drilled yet will produce as much oil as those that have been drilled. But a lot of the land leased to oil companies has already been explored and was found not to have enough recoverable oil to justify drilling. So it makes no sense to assume that the unused acres would produce as much oil as the acres already used. At the same time, 97 percent of offshore areas haven't been leased to oil companies yet, and we know there are billions of barrels of oil in these areas.

ARGUMENT AGAINST MORE AMERICAN ENERGY NOW

Oil companies should be required to use the lands already available for drilling or lose the rights to them. Such a "use it or lose it" system would lead to a greater supply of oil while keeping in place the current bans to protect offshore areas.

REBUTTAL

This unfair policy is based on faulty assumptions. First, oil companies are already required by the 1992 Comprehensive Energy Act to do all they can to develop the areas leased to them. Otherwise, they lose the lease. Randall Luthi, Director of the MMS, recently made it clear that if oil companies are not making significant progress on their leases "and I do mean significant progress toward actually producing—those leases come back and we sell them again." As Congressman Gene Green (D-TX) recently pointed out, a "use it or lose it" requirement is redundant and will do nothing to increase supply since companies are already doing all they can to produce oil where it makes sense to do so on available land.

Second, this proposal is based on the idea that drilling will be profitable when it's carried out on any random piece of leased land. But most land does not contain enough oil to justify the investment it takes to produce oil from it. It takes millions and sometimes billions of dollars to verify whether an oil well has enough oil to be worth drilling, and there is no guarantee that it will be. Only one in three onshore wells contains enough oil to make it commercially viable, and only one in five offshore wells has enough oil to warrant commercial drilling. Thus, it makes no sense for oil companies to start drilling on every acre of land. A "use it or lose it" requirement will not incentivize oil companies to drill more, as they will continue to drill only where it's likely to be profitable.

Third, it's unfair for Congress to require oil companies to drill according to some arbitrary deadline or timetable when the regulatory and legal obstacles to drilling that Congress has put in place slow down companies' efforts to begin producing oil. For example, legal challenges to lease sales in the Rocky Mountains have risen from 27 percent of all leases in 2001 to 81 percent in 2007, according to government and industry records. These legal battles can drag on for some time. Congress can't expect oil companies to drill faster when it keeps making it harder to drill.

ARGUMENT AGAINST MORE
AMERICAN ENERGY NOW

Drilling in ANWR would destroy a pristine wilderness.

REBUTTAL

Dramatic advances in technology have made it possible to drill in ANWR without causing any significant damage to the environment. We can drill while using a lot less area than was previously the case. For example, when the Prudhoe Bay drilling facilities in Alaska were constructed in the 1970s, gravel was laid down over 2 percent of the field for use in roads and drilling and production sites. Because of technological innovations, however, Prudhoe Bay could be developed today with 60 percent less land covered.

Similarly, in the 1970s production pads had to be spaced 100 feet or more apart, but new technologies allow for them to occupy much less space. A number of drills that would have once required sixty-five acres now only need nine, a sharp reduction in land usage.

To further minimize the human impact of drilling, oil companies have developed roads made from ice for use during winter. These roads dissolve when the weather warms up.

These are just a few of the examples of the dramatic technological achievements that will allow drilling in ANWR to be conducted safely and with minimal disruption of local wildlife.

ARGUMENT AGAINST MORE
AMERICAN ENERGY NOW

Drilling for more oil will keep us "addicted to oil" and prevent us from moving on to renewable and cleaner technologies. We should focus on shifting to new technologies rather than focusing on old ones.

REBUTTAL

This argument is fundamentally dishonest and assumes a false, unnecessary choice. We don't have to choose between investing in new technology and investing in our oil supplies. We can invest in new technologies and plan for a transition to new fuels while at the same time using the resources we have now to deal with the current energy crisis. The only thing preventing us from doing this is misguided government policies.

The idea that drilling for more oil keeps us "addicted" to oil and prevents us from moving on to new technologies makes absolutely no sense. If a new alternative fuel were to be developed that cost the same as or slightly less than oil, was renewable, and was accessible to the market, it would replace oil as our primary energy source faster than you can imagine.

The truth is that as soon as a viable and competitive alternative fuel is developed, Americans will respond by moving away from oil.

ARGUMENT AGAINST MORE
AMERICAN ENERGY NOW

Offshore drilling platforms dump vast amounts of mercury and other dangerous metals into the ocean. More drilling will lead to more mercury in the oceans and a greater threat to marine and human life.

REBUTTAL

Research has shown that the amount of mercury involved in offshore drilling poses no significant threat to marine or human life, and that the levels of mercury and methylmercury in marine organisms around offshore platforms is not elevated compared to those far away from platforms. It's also notable that the amount of mercury entering the Gulf of Mexico from offshore drilling is only 0.7 percent of the amount of mercury that enters the Gulf from the Mississippi River.

ARGUMENT AGAINST MORE
AMERICAN ENERGY NOW

Offshore drilling requires the use of seismic surveys for exploration that harm whales and fish.

REBUTTAL

Research has shown both that seismic surveys pose no danger to many studied fish populations, and that fish would not experience hearing damage because they avoid areas where seismic surveys are taking place. While whales might be displaced by seismic surveys, this condition is temporary and the whales return once the seismic activity stops.

Additionally, there is absolutely no firm evidence that seismic surveys permanently harm whale hearing or cause strandings. Evidence suggests that for almost every species of marine mammal the risk of temporary hearing damage is not significant.

In general, seismic surveys are not a significant problem for the marine environment. Of course, we must always be careful and make sure we have the right rules in place, but current regulations more than adequately protect marine wildlife.

ARGUMENT AGAINST MORE AMERICAN ENERGY NOW

More drilling offshore will lead to oil spills that will damage wildlife and beaches.

REBUTTAL

In fact, there hasn't been a major spill from offshore drilling since 1980. Ninety-seven percent of all oil spills from drilling is one barrel or less of oil. The Royal Society of Canada did a review of the annual risk of a large oil spill resulting from offshore drilling and found that the chances were about 1 in 10,000, or 0.0001 percent per well.

The risk of a significant spill from an oil tanker in U.S. waters is also remote, and the chances of a major spill from drilling are even lower. MMS data shows that for every 1 billion barrels of oil transported by tankers in U.S. waters from 1985 to 1999, there were just 0.73 spills of 1,000 barrels or more.

ARGUMENT AGAINST MORE AMERICAN ENERGY NOW

Drilling for oil shale in Colorado, Utah, and Wyoming would be environmentally destructive. It would endanger several important species and pollute the air and water.

REBUTTAL

Shell Oil Company has pioneered a new process for obtaining oil from shale called in situ (on site) extraction. The rock is heated underground to the point where the oil is released and can be pumped back to the surface. This process would use a lot less land than we would have had to use years ago with on-surface mining. The impact on wildlife would also be greatly reduced.

Of course, any kind of development will have an impact on wildlife and the land, just as oil and gas drilling does today. However, with oil and gas we have developed stringent environmental standards that have succeeded in safeguarding endangered species and protecting important habitat. The same can be done for oil shale.

There is no evidence that oil shale will significantly reduce air quality. In fact, the only studies we have on this problem indicate that air quality standards could be met. Those studies, which are from the 1970s and 1980s, were conducted using old technology and processes, and it's reasonable to expect that advances in technology since then would make oil shale development even safer for the air. The truth is that no one can make any definitive claims about this until new studies are carried out.

As for water quality, Shell's new in situ process protects the water table by creating an ice barrier around the affected area. This forms an impermeable barrier that prevents chemicals and oil from seeping down into the water table. Shell is conducting trials of this technique, but it is confident it can protect water quality.

ARGUMENT AGAINST MORE AMERICAN ENERGY NOW

In order to fight climate change, we must not do anything that will contribute any more carbon into the atmosphere. Instead, we should adopt a cap-and-trade system similar to the one proposed in the Boxer-Warner-Lieberman bill.

REBUTTAL

The first thing we have to understand is that a system of regulation and taxation will not help solve the problem of climate change. This is because reducing the amount of carbon in the atmosphere requires an international solution. If the U.S. and Europe adopt a cap-and-trade system or a carbon tax, the total effect will be negligent so long as China, India, and poor nations continue to dump increasing amounts of carbon into the atmosphere. And developing nations have made clear that they will never implement carbon-cutting measures that hurt their economies.

The only realistic way to address concerns about climate change is to invent new technologies and improvements in efficiency that the entire world will voluntarily adopt. Developing these kinds of technologies will require a lot of money, the kind that can only be found in a strong economy. And a regulation and taxation system on carbon would be devastating to our economy, since every sector of the economy uses carbon. Ironically, such a system would undermine our very ability to address climate change.

The best way to address climate change challenges is to have a strong economy that gives us the ability to invent technology to reduce our carbon emissions. And because a strong economy requires plentiful energy, we have to do all we can now to develop all American energy sources while working on new ways to address carbon emissions.

By committing ourselves to a strategy of more American energy, more economic growth, and more advanced technology, we'll find a way to cut our emissions faster than we ever thought possible. The answer is innovation and technology, not taxation and regulation.

AMERICAN SOLUTIONS FOR WINNING THE FUTURE

THE MORE AMERICAN ENERGY NOW "FIRST STEPS" PLEDGE

FEDERAL OFFICE HOLDERS AND CANDIDATES

IN ORDER TO help every American whose family finances are strained or job is threatened by the energy crisis, and to strengthen the American economy; and

RECOGNIZING that more than 1.4 million Americans have signed the American Solutions "Drill Now, Drill Here, Pay Less" petition that calls on the U.S. Congress to act immediately to lower gasoline, diesel, and other fuel prices by authorizing the exploration of American energy resources to reduce our dependence on foreign energy resources from unstable countries:

I, _____, **THEREFORE** pledge to the citizens of the _____ district of the State of _____ and to the American People that I will take the following first steps in producing more American energy now:

ONE, support ending the federal ban on offshore drilling for oil and natural gas and giving coastal states the right to choose whether to begin drilling off their shores;

TWO, support ending the federal ban on drilling for oil and natural gas in the Alaskan National Wildlife Refuge (ANWR); and

THREE, support ending all prohibitions on the development of the more than 800 billion barrels of oil shale in Colorado, Utah, Wyoming, and the rest of the United States.

Signed   _____

Date _____

Witness   _____

Witness   _____

State Office Holders and Candidates

IN ORDER TO help every American and every citizen of this state whose family finances are strained or job is threatened by the energy crisis, strengthen the American economy and the economy of this state which is weakened by high inflation due to high energy prices, and reduce this state's and America's dependence on foreign energy sources:

I, _____, pledge to the citizens of the _____ district of the State of _____ and to all the people of this state, that I will support any and all efforts to increase the development in this state of American energy resources, including—in those states where it applies—the exploration and development of oil and natural gas resources offshore our state's coastlines.

Signed _____

Date _____

Witness   _____

Witness   _____

HOW RISING GAS PRICES AFFECT YOUR FAMILY'S BUDGET

FAMILY GASOLINE COSTS BASED ON MILES DRIVEN, GAS PRICES, AND MILEAGE

Miles Driven Per Year (@ 15 MPG)

Gas Prices	5,000	7,500	10,000	12,500	15,000	17,500	20,000
$ 5.50	$ 1,833	$ 2,750	$ 3,667	$ 4,583	$ 5,500	$ 6,417	$ 7,333
$ 5.40	$ 1,800	$ 2,700	$ 3,600	$ 4,500	$ 5,400	$ 6,300	$ 7,200
$ 5.20	$ 1,733	$ 2,600	$ 3,467	$ 4,333	$ 5,200	$ 6,067	$ 6,933
$ 5.00	$ 1,667	$ 2,500	$ 3,333	$ 4,167	$ 5,000	$ 5,833	$ 6,667
$ 4.80	$ 1,600	$ 2,400	$ 3,200	$ 4,000	$ 4,800	$ 5,600	$ 6,400
$ 4.60	$ 1,533	$ 2,300	$ 3,067	$ 3,833	$ 4,600	$ 5,367	$ 6,133
$ 4.50	$ 1,500	$ 2,250	$ 3,000	$ 3,750	$ 4,500	$ 5,250	$ 6,000
$ 4.40	$ 1,467	$ 2,200	$ 2,933	$ 3,667	$ 4,400	$ 5,133	$ 5,867
$ 4.20	$ 1,400	$ 2,100	$ 2,800	$ 3,500	$ 4,200	$ 4,900	$ 5,600
$ 4.00	$ 1,333	$ 2,000	$ 2,667	$ 3,333	$ 4,000	$ 4,667	$ 5,333

Miles Driven Per Year (@ 20 MPG)

Gas Prices	5,000	7,500	10,000	12,500	15,000	17,500	20,000
$ 5.50	$ 1,375	$ 2,063	$ 2,750	$ 3,438	$ 4,125	$ 4,813	$ 5,500
$ 5.40	$ 1,350	$ 2,025	$ 2,700	$ 3,375	$ 4,050	$ 4,725	$ 5,400
$ 5.20	$ 1,300	$ 1,950	$ 2,600	$ 3,250	$ 3,900	$ 4,550	$ 5,200
$ 5.00	$ 1,250	$ 1,875	$ 2,500	$ 3,125	$ 3,750	$ 4,375	$ 5,000
$ 4.80	$ 1,200	$ 1,800	$ 2,400	$ 3,000	$ 3,600	$ 4,200	$ 4,800
$ 4.60	$ 1,150	$ 1,725	$ 2,300	$ 2,875	$ 3,450	$ 4,025	$ 4,600
$ 4.50	$ 1,125	$ 1,688	$ 2,250	$ 2,813	$ 3,375	$ 3,938	$ 4,500
$ 4.40	$ 1,100	$ 1,650	$ 2,200	$ 2,750	$ 3,300	$ 3,850	$ 4,400
$ 4.20	$ 1,050	$ 1,575	$ 2,100	$ 2,625	$ 3,150	$ 3,675	$ 4,200
$ 4.00	$ 1,000	$ 1,500	$ 2,000	$ 2,500	$ 3,000	$ 3,500	$ 4,000

Miles Driven Per Year (@ 30 MPG)

Gas Prices	5,000	7,500	10,000	12,500	15,000	17,500	20,000
$ 5.50	$ 917	$ 1,375	$ 1,833	$ 2,292	$ 2,750	$ 3,208	$ 3,667
$ 5.40	$ 900	$ 1,350	$ 1,800	$ 2,250	$ 2,700	$ 3,150	$ 3,600
$ 5.20	$ 867	$ 1,300	$ 1,733	$ 2,167	$ 2,600	$ 3,033	$ 3,467
$ 5.00	$ 833	$ 1,250	$ 1,667	$ 2,083	$ 2,500	$ 2,917	$ 3,333
$ 4.80	$ 800	$ 1,200	$ 1,600	$ 2,000	$ 2,400	$ 2,800	$ 3,200
$ 4.60	$ 767	$ 1,150	$ 1,533	$ 1,917	$ 2,300	$ 2,683	$ 3,067
$ 4.50	$ 750	$ 1,125	$ 1,500	$ 1,875	$ 2,250	$ 2,625	$ 3,000
$ 4.40	$ 733	$ 1,100	$ 1,467	$ 1,833	$ 2,200	$ 2,567	$ 2,933
$ 4.20	$ 700	$ 1,050	$ 1,400	$ 1,750	$ 2,100	$ 2,450	$ 2,800
$ 4.00	$ 667	$ 1,000	$ 1,333	$ 1,667	$ 2,000	$ 2,333	$ 2,667

ACKNOWLEDGMENTS

All my creative efforts are only made possible through the support of these institutions: the American Enterprise Institute and its leader, Chris DeMuth; the Center for Health Transformation and its leader, Nancy Desmond; Gingrich Communications and its leader, Kathy Lubbers; American Solutions and its leader Dave Ryan; Gingrich Productions led by Callista Gingrich; and Sonya Harrison, leader of the Office of Speaker Newt Gingrich.

Developing the ideas and concepts in *Drill Here, Drill Now, Pay Less* has been a work of a lifetime executed in real time. The list of everyone who helped shape this book should include hundreds of people. However, there are key individuals who truly made this book possible, and they need to be acknowledged for their help with thinking, writing, and editing.

At AEI, I owe a debt of gratitude to the generosity of Ken and Yvonne Hannan and the president, Chris DeMuth. In my AEI office specifically, Vince and I want to acknowledge Emily Renwick who helped keep everything orderly throughout the book process and without whose cheerful can-do attitude this book probably would not have been finished on time; Steve Everley, who tackled cataloging the vast collection of America's energy resources; and our summer interns Joel Alicea, Jennifer Marsico, and Jennifer Souers, whose contributions were invaluable. Joel in particular played a major role in helping us understand the scholarship on the environmental impact of offshore drilling as well as the complex array of regulatory and litigation obstacles to developing America's energy resources. Joel also deserves credit for helping the public better understand the relationship between opening up new areas for oil and gas exploration off our coasts and in Alaska, and the impact such a change in law would have on lowering our fuel prices today.

AEI also sustains a number of experts who have been very helpful in this project including David Gerson, Kevin Hassett, and Arthur Brooks (whom we welcome to AEI as the new president this January). We have been very fortunate to work the last year with Navy Capt. Donald Cuddington, who played an important role in helping us understand the extraordinary productive capacity the United States unleashed during World War II.

Vince and I were able to rely, as always, on my dear friend and primary mentor Steve Hanser, who kept pushing us to think carefully and write clearly and was once again at the center of this project. In everything I do, I must enlist the advice and involvement of my friend and strategist, Randy Evans, without whom this book would not have been written. My daughter, Jackie Cushman, has given me the joy of two grandchildren, who bring the future and the significance of this book sharply into focus.

The American Solutions team executed the "Drill Here, Drill Now, Pay Less" petition drive and really brought the issue of more American energy now to national prominence. We thank: Joe Gaylord, a co-designer of the Contract with America and the 1994 campaign, who is now leading our efforts at American Solutions; Dave Ryan, the American Solutions president, who has led the petition drive to over 1.4 million signatures; Pat Saks, vice president and COO, without whom American Solutions could not function; finance director Dorinda Moss and Amy Pass, her outstanding right hand; Michael Krull as director of education and Fred Asbell as coalition coordinator, who have been very helpful, as has Christine Hall and Princella Smith, spokesperson for the Platform of the American People; and press secretary Dan Kotman, Adam Waldeck, David Kralik, Tim Cameron, AJ Young, and Paul Kilgore. Contributing interns this summer include Alexander Kisling, Brad Griff, Katie Kerl, Jessica Paulson, and Kyle Johnson

On behalf of the Lubbers Agency: Kathy Lubbers and Randy Evans did a great job of representing us in the book negotiation and production. Marji Ross, president of Regnery Publishing, has been extraordinary in her dedication to getting *Drill Here, Drill Now, Pay Less* right and in supporting the speed it took to write and publish the manuscript in real time.

Harry Crocker influenced much of the direction and framing of the book and Jack Langer at Regnery did a superb job of editing under a very tough deadline and making the book a much better read. Jeff Carneal, the president of Eagle Publishing, continued to exhort and encourage both the growth of my weekly e-newsletter, "Winning the Future," and my book, *Real Change*.

Once again, Stefan Passantino and Anthony Morris brought their legal talents to bear. In addition, my daughter Jackie Cushman provided innumerable suggestions for improvement and invention.

Polling played an important role in ensuring we thoroughly understood the values and concerns of the American people. Specifically, pollsters David Winston, Kellyanne Conway, Frank Luntz, and Jim Clifton (the head of Gallup, the largest and most prestigious polling institution in the world) have been invaluable. On American opinion, Karlyn Bowman at AEI is extremely knowledgeable and a thoughtful analyst and scholar. All helped us focus on the language and intensity of the issues in this book.

The Gingrich Communications Team: led by president Kathy Lubbers; Rick Tyler, my superb spokesperson; Joe DeSantis, communications director; Jessica Gavora, a tremendously gifted writer who helps with my weekly newsletter and assisted with parts of this book; Michelle Selesky, who helped coordinate with outside reviewers to look over specific sections and is managing the "transforming energy solution" section of our online offer along with Matt Scofield, who will continue to assist with the online effort. Summer interns include Catherine Butterworth, Jillian Lane, Melissa Chambers, and Olivia Blanchard, who helped to collect personal stories about the impact of high gas prices.

We decided at the end of June that we wanted to complement our book efforts with a movie so we turned to Dave Bossie to help put together a one-hour film about the energy challenges facing America and the solutions we need as a country to overcome them. Putting together a film on a tight schedule is never easy, but Dave, directors Terry Moloney, and Kevin Knoblock, along with the team that Dave leads at Citizens United, including Michael Boos, Lauren Fleming, Jennifer Laurence, Dain Valverde, and Matthew Taylor, have responded magnificently. It would not be as much fun filming if it weren't for Rhonda Jenkins and Dave's son, Griffin, who joined us in filming along the way.

Sean Hannity deserves tremendous credit for his national leadership in advocating the "Drill Here, Drill Now, Pay Less" petition, and we also thank Neal Boortz, who has encouraged all our efforts.

Terry Balderson, Lou Pugliarsi, Bill Forstchen, Fredrick Palmer, Bob Walker, Terry Maple, David Bockorny, Cliff May, and Anne Korin all helped in critiquing various sections of the book. Economics Professor R. Morris Coats of Nicholls State University was also a tremendous help in explaining the relationship of long-term supply increases to current oil prices. Glenn Vawter, executive director of National Oil Shale Association, and Dr. Jeremy Boak of the Center for Oil Shale Technology and Research of the Colorado School of Mines, each added their expertise to our understanding of oil shale. Augie Pitrolo, a thirty-year veteran of the Department of Energy, also provided critical feedback on our proposed solutions.

Michael Williams, chairman of the Texas Railroad Commission, provided excellent critique and his outstanding leadership in Texas on energy and other issues is a tremendous inspiration. Dan Kish of the Institute for Energy Research, an institution that does great work advancing understanding of the need for more American energy, also provided invaluable comments on the manuscript.

Annette Guarisco, Keith Cole, and Ken Cole at General Motors have been helpful throughout the years in understanding the challenges facing America's auto industry and in thinking through some of the required solutions. Roger Herrera, president of Northern Knowledge and a foremost expert on the Alaskan National Wildlife Refuge, helped us understand the issues involved in drilling in ANWR. Enid Borden, president and CEO of Meals-on-Wheels, understands all too well the real human impact of high energy prices on vulnerable Americans who depend on their neighbors as volunteers to drive the long miles to bring them a daily meal.

If not for the strong support from the Office of Speaker Newt Gingrich, the many projects I am engaged in would collapse. Sonya Harrison does an amazing job keeping track of all our activities and schedules, and she is ably assisted by Bess Kelly and Heather Favors. In addition, an invaluable asset to the Office of Speaker Newt Gingrich is Lindsey Harvey, my special assistant and chief coordinator for tasking and operations.

The most encouraging development in our American Solutions movement for more American energy now has been the number of elected officials who have actively sought to develop more energy at lower cost for the American people.

Senators Lamar Alexander, John Barrasso, Richard Burr, and Bob Corker were among the first to ask us to look at a new energy strategy. House leader John Boehner, whip Roy Blunt, and key activists like Eric Cantor, Kevin McCarthy, Paul Ryan, Michael Burgess, Mike Pence, Lyn Westmoreland, and Tom Price were invaluable. The "All of the Above" energy bill introduced by Boehner and House Republicans is a model of the "Do it all, Do it now, Do it for America" approach we've been advocating at American Solutions.

Finally, I'd like to thank my wife Callista, who has enhanced this book tremendously. Co-starring in our new energy movie, We Have the Power, Callista has kept her eye on that script and the dual impact that the book and the movie will have on the future of American energy as we launch both projects this fall on Solutions Day, September 27. Our work together at Gingrich Productions beginning with our films *Rediscovering God in America* and *Rendezvous with Destiny*, a documentary about the presidency of Ronald Reagan, has made this journey even more enjoyable.

NOTES

CHAPTER TWO

1. Http://www.latimes.com/news/nationworld/nation/lana-drilling15-2008jul15,0,1214318.story.

2. Http://ipl.unm.edu/cwl/fedbook/anilca.html.

3. Http://www.biologicaldiversity.org/news/press_releases/beaufort oil-00-15-2007.html.

4. Http://www.blm.gov/wo/st/en/prog/energy/oil_and_gas/EPCA_III/EPCA_III_faq.html.

5. Http://www.ipaa.org/news/wr/WR-2000-04-30.pdf.

6. Http://www.tucsoncitizen.com/daily/local/19103.php.

7. Http://www.arizonacleanfuels.com/news/2008/020508_YS.htm.

8. Http://www.rediff.com/money/2007/nov/27hub.htm.

9. Http://www.blm.gov/wo/st/en/info/newsroom/2008/July/NR_07_02_2008.html.

10. Http://www.nytimes.com/2008/06/25/business/25dow.html.

11. This and other energy-related polls can be viewed at AmericanSolutions.com.

CHAPTER THREE

1. Http://www.blm.gov/wo/st/en/prog/energy/oil_and_gas/EPCA_III.html.

2. Http://www.mms.gov/revaldiv/PDFs/FinalInvRptToCongress050106.pdf

3. Table 1, http://fpc.state.gov/documents/organization/107225.pdf.

4. Http://www.usgs.gov/newsroom/article.asp?ID=1980&from=rss_home.

5. Http://www.heritage.org/Research/EnergyandEnvironment/bg2086.cfm.

6. Http://nei.org/filefolder/US_Electricity_Production_Costs.ppt.

7. Http://nei.org/filefolder/US_Nuclear_Industrial_Safety_Accident_Rate_1.ppt.

8. Http://nuclear.inl.gov/docs/factsheets/radiation_safety_nuclear_power_plants_1003.pdf.

9. Http://www.hillsdale.edu/news/imprimis/archive/issue.asp?year=2008&month=02.

10. Http://www.world-nuclear.org/info/inf36.html.

11. Http://www.gen-4.org/.

12. Http://www.eia.doe.gov/mer/pdf/pages/sec2_13.pdf.

13. Http://fossil.energy.gov/education/energylessons/coal/gen_coal.html.

14. Http://news-service.stanford.edu/news/2005/may25/wind-052505.html.

15. Http://www1.eere.energy.gov/biomass/biomass_basics_faqs.html.

16. Http://www.ethanolproducer.com/article.jsp?article_id=4466.

17. Http://www.eere.energy.gov/afdc/fuels/stations_counts.html.

18. Http://www.eere.energy.gov/afdc/fuels/stations_counts.html.

CHAPTER FIVE

1. National Academy of Sciences. *Oil in the Sea: Inputs, Fates, and Effects.* National Research Council. Washington, DC: National Academies Press, 2003.

2. Royal Society of Canada. *Report of the Expert Panel on Science Issues Related to Oil and Gas Activities, Offshore British Columbia.* Natural Resources Canada. Ottawa, 2004.

3. U.S. Coast Guard. *Draft PEIS: Vessel and Facility Response Plans for Oil: 2003 Removal Equipment Requirements and Alternative Technology Revisions.* While some areas in those three re-

gions will undoubtedly be more sensitive to oil spills than the Coast Guard modeling suggests because the modeling was not strictly representative, the study gives us a good idea of the environmental risks of an oil spill.

4. Peterson, David L. *Background Briefing Paper for a Workshop on Seismic Survey Operations: Impacts on Fish, Fisheries, Fishers and Aquaculture.* British Columbia Seafood Alliance. 2004.

5. Dalen, John, Egil Dragsund, et al. *Effects of Seismic Surveys on Fish, Fish Catches, and Sea Mammals.* Cooperation Group-Fishery Industry and Petroleum Industry. DNV Energy, 2007.

6. Abgrall, Patrick, Valerie Moulton, and W J. Richardson. *Updated Review of Scientific Information on Impacts of Seismic Survey Sound on Marine Mammals, 2004-Present.* Department of Fisheries and Oceans, Habitat Science Branch. LGL Limited, Environmental Research Associates, 2008.

7. Minerals Management Service. *Estimated Petroleum Spillage From Facilities Associated with Federal Outer Continental Shelf (OCS) Oil and Gas Activities Resulting From Damages Caused by Hurricanes Rita and Katrina in 2005.* Department of Interior, 2006.

8. "MMS Prepares for 2008 Hurricane Season." MMS Press Release. May 15, 2008. Http://www.gomr.mms.gov/homepg/whatsnew/newsreal/2008/080515.pdf.

9. Http://www.doi.gov/news/03_News_Releases/030311.htm.

10. Http://www.instituteforenergyresearch.org/anwr/.

11. Http://www.doi.gov/anwr/.

12. Http://www.rand.org/pubs/monographs/2005/RAND_MG414.sum.pdf.

13. Http://www.nrc.gov/reading-rm/doc-collections/fact-sheets/3mile-isle.html.

14. Http://www.world-nuclear.org/info/inf36.html.

15. Http://www.quinnipiac.edu/x2882.xml?ReleaseID=1196.

WHAT ARE YOU WAITING FOR?
JOIN THE MOVEMENT!

Sign this card to join the 1 million-plus people demanding more American energy now.

The American Solutions
Coalition for More American Energy Now
Membership Requirements

1. I have read the *Drill Here, Drill Now, Pay Less* handbook.

2. I have joined the movement for more American energy now by signing the "Drill Here, Drill Now, Pay Less" petition at www.AmericanSolutions.com.

3. I will strongly urge elected officials and candidates to take the first steps to develop more American energy now by lifting the federal bans on oil and natural gas drilling offshore and in Alaska, and by overturning the ban on oil shale development in Colorado, Utah, and Wyoming.

DRILL HERE
DRILL NOW
PAY LESS

www.AmericanSolutions.com

For more information on the solutions, facts, and arguments contained in *Drill Here, Drill Now, Pay Less*, visit:

www.AmericanSolutions.com/EnergyHandbook
www.Newt.org/EnergyHandbook

To see a trailer of Newt and Callista Gingrich's movie on energy, *We Have The Power*, visit:

www.WeHaveThePowerMovie.com